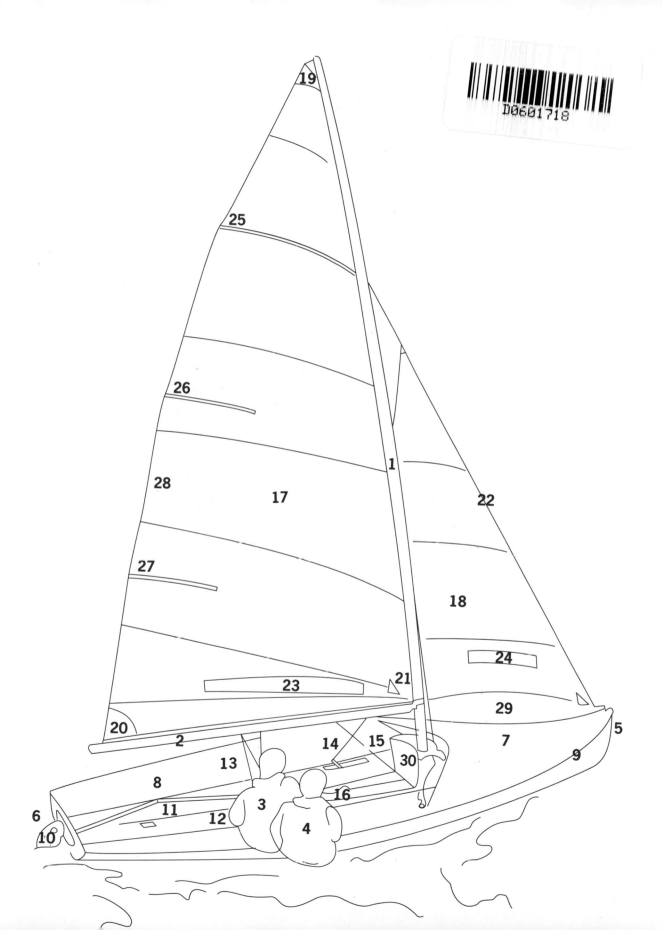

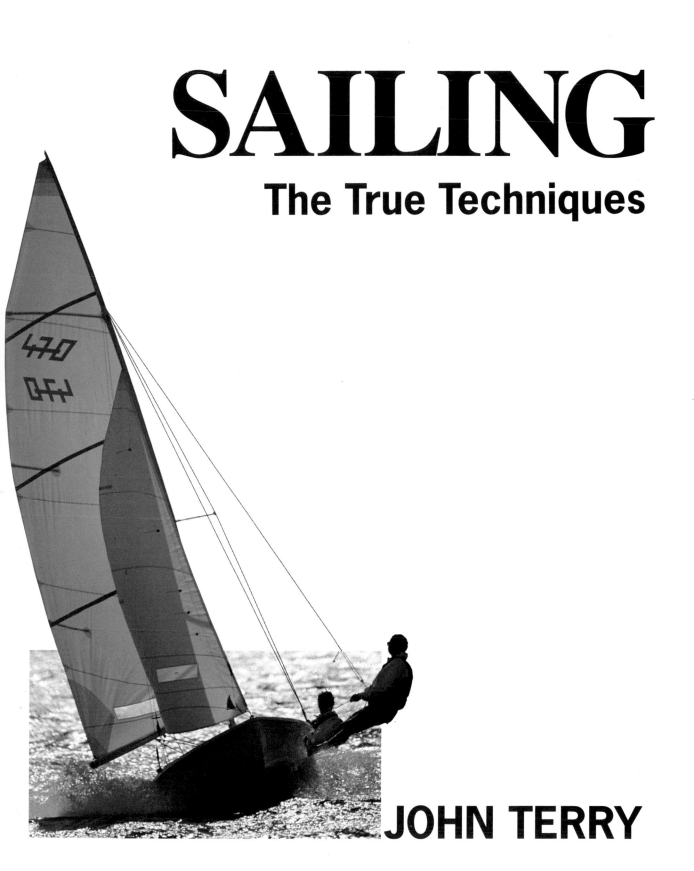

SAILING
The True Techniques

JOHN TERRY

First published 1991

Copyright © 1991 Elm Grove Books Limited
Text copyright © 1991 John Terry
The right of John Terry to be identified as the author
of this work has been asserted by him in accordance
with the Copyright, Design and Patents Act, 1988.

A CIP record for this book is available upon request
from the British Library.

This edition published in 1993 by
Bloomsbury Books an imprint of
The Godfrey Cave Group
42 Bloomsbury Street, London WC1B 3QJ
under license from Elm Grove Books Limited

ISBN 1 85471 173 3

Printed and bound in Spain

Acknowledgements

The *470* sailors: Paul Brotherton, the British *470* National Champion 1991, and Vanessa Weedon-Jones. The *J24* sailors: Peter Eastman, Andrew Kerr, Chris Peterson, Tony Rey, Joan Touchette, Max Williamson. The Sailboarders: Miguel Bruggerman, John Hoots.

My special thanks to Paul Brotherton and Vanessa Weedon-Jones for being so helpful, patient, and understanding. Also to Edward Hyde, David Jeffrie and the staff of Hyde Sails for supplying the *470* sails and allowing us to photograph their sail loft.

I am indebted to the following for their help in many ways:
Racing Sailboats Ltd; The London Yacht Centre; Tim Duffy of J World, Key West Florida; Totos Theodossiou and Michael Grontides, Limassol Nautical Club; The Royal Yachting Association; Cyprus Yachting Association; Captain Henry Wrigley, Harbour Master, Cowes Harbour Commission; Henri Lloyd; Michael Dixon; Philip Everard; Nigel Harley; John McIntosh; Anthony Parkes; and Jane Terry.

Additional photography
Allsports p 131; Beken of Cowes 8TL, 9BR, 128-129, 132-133, 134-135, 136-137B, 138-139T, 143, 145T; Roger Lean-Vercoe 145-146, 147, 148-149; John Terry 3, 8BL, 9L, 150,151.

Contents

Introduction

I remember well the thrill of being able to sail a boat on my own for the first time. It was easier than rowing, and I felt I could go anywhere. I still feel that one of the main attractions of sailing is the ability to reach a destination using only the natural force of the wind.

I learnt to sail in *Cadets* which have three sails and a crew of two, and every year we raced at Burnham on Crouch with experts lecturing us on our mistakes in the evening. It was a wonderful way to learn. Later, at University, I graduated to the sport of team racing where teams of three dinghies raced against each other. Individual position mattered less than the overall position of the team, and here I acquired a good grounding in tactics. There were the occasional times when we abandoned our dinghies for a trip across the Channel to France in larger cruising boats. Cruising itself has many attractions, but, when I am sailing off-shore I still prefer to race. I enjoy the company, the competition and the celebrations at the end, particularly after a long race like the Fastnet.

Of course, there are times when it's great just to potter around. One of my happier memories is when we spent a wonderful evening, loaded up with cans of beer, just drifting in the wind watching the sun set over Key West in Florida. We'd been sailing all day in the *J24* doing photography for this book, and you would have thought we might have had enough of boats!

The *Flying Fifteen* is another racing keel boat that I was introduced to by the inimitable Uffa Fox for whom I used to crew in 'Coweslip'. And I still own one, though I have to admit that my love for speed and excitement is better served now by my catamaran or by sailboards. Even so, recent developments of modern sails and lightweight hull construction have produced some exciting craft such as the *470* that features in this book.

The variety of sailing is a continual delight. You can go cruising off-shore or pottering up creeks. You can race boats of all types and sizes. You can sail inland on lakes and rivers, or you can contend with the waves and currents of the sea. You can sail fast, lively boats or slow comfortable ones. The weather, too, provides a constant challenge – coaxing your boat along in the merest zephyr one day, and keeping it driving in a strong wind the next. There are magic days when the sun shines and the wind blows perfectly, and others when you are wet and cold and wish you had never gone out.

When I learnt to sail, it was largely by trial and error – and I made a lot of mistakes. I hope that in this book I will have shown you how to avoid some of them. Though, in the end, practical experience is the only way to achieve any degree of mastery.

If I were asked to sum up what I felt to be the most important element of sailing skill, I would say that it would be to have a strong sense of feel and balance so that keeping your boat in trim and responding to your wishes becomes almost second nature. Having to fight against the force of the wind and the pull of the sails makes sailing a battle rather than a joyful challenge. The theory of how wind and water act on a boat can only be applied with practice, and only then will you really feel when a boat is balanced and sailing comfortably. But the second most important element in successful sailing is being able to use your eyes, so that you can exploit a situation or avoid a potential problem.

There is real satisfaction in sailing a boat well. I hope this book will help you achieve it.

The development of sailing

The four examples here, show how sailing has developed from the old design of the square-rigger and the J-class yacht to the modern off-shore racing yacht and the catamaran.

EAGLE is a 294-foot long square-rigged American sail training ship used to give experience to the cadets of the US Coastguard. The square rig was used on all large commercial sailing ships during the last century. With the wind blowing from the quarter, this rig produces considerable power, and *EAGLE* can attain quite a high speed if the conditions are right. However, when the wind is blowing closer to her bow she cannot sail anywhere near as close to it as can a yacht like *VELSHEDA* which has a modern fore and aft rig.

VELSHEDA is a J-class yacht, the class that was developed in the 1930s for racing in the America's Cup. She was built by Camper & Nicholson of Gosport in 1933 and her steel hull displaces 205 tons. She is 127 feet overall, 83 feet on the waterline, and carries 7,600 square feet of sail. She never competed for the America's Cup but raced for several years in the British regatta circuit. Though she lay neglected for many years she has now been restored and

The square-rigged *EAGLE* (left)
The J-class *VELSHEDA* (below)

can still be seen sailing in the Solent.

In *VELSHEDA's* heyday few people took part in recreational sailing, and racing a J-class yacht required a large number of professional crewmen and a very healthy bank balance. Nowadays, sailing is one of the world's most popular sports. Modern design and materials have enormously simplified the management of a boat and has brought the pastime of dinghy racing within reach of nearly everyone.

Cruiser

The catamaran is another design of modern sailing boat that has become increasingly popular. The speeds they can attain make them exhilarating to handle. In the right conditions some types, like the Dart design shown here, can actually sail faster than the wind driving them. They have very light, narrow hulls that cut cleanly through the water leaving little wash behind them. They can carry a large sail area because the crew can exert great leverage with their weight to prevent excessive heeling.

In each of these four examples, the sailor uses the interaction of wind and water on his craft to drive it along. The boats may be different but the principles are the same. In this book we have used three different types of boat to demonstrate the fundamentals and techniques of sailing. They are introduced overleaf.

Catamaran

However, ocean racing is expensive and your pocket still has to be pretty deep before you can afford a yacht like *TRUMPETER* pictured here setting her multi-coloured spinnaker. She is an example of the 46-foot long Swan class and is fast to sail and yet has comfortable living accommodation below deck. Yachts of this type have powerful winches to make sail handling easier and they can race over long distances.

Introducing the dinghy, the keel boat and the windsurfer

The dinghy used in this book is the *470*. It was designed by André Corny in 1965 and is a typical modern racing dinghy whose rig has developed over the years. Competition is keen in this class because it is used for the Olympic Games. The length of the *470* is 4.7 metres and its beam, or width, is 1.68 metres. It has a retractable centreboard, and so can be sailed right into the beach. It carries sails which total 12.7 square metres in area and this is almost doubled when the huge, 12.5 square-metre spinnaker is hoisted.

A dinghy is always sailed as upright as possible, though the force of the wind in the sails will make it heel. To counter-balance this heeling the crew sit out as far as possible on the windward side. If the wind increases too much, there are ways of bending the mast and altering the shape of the mainsail which can control the amount of wind in it. In really strong winds there is always the risk that a dinghy may capsize, so it is not wise to venture out without some rescue cover. A motor rescue boat should be provided for those racing by the sailing club organising the event.

Many of the top ocean racing fraternity start their careers in sailing dinghies and as most people are first taught to sail a dinghy, so the *470* is used here to demonstrate all the basic techniques of sailing. It is a very responsive boat and is therefore excellent for demonstrating the effect of changes in sail trim and weight distribution.

The keel boat used in this book is the *J24* lightweight cruiser/racer. Designed by Rod Johnson, it is 7.32 metres long with a beam of 2.72 metres. It is called a keel boat because it has a fixed keel which requires a minimum depth of 1.22 metres of water. It has high

In strong winds the crew reduce the working size of the mainsail by reefing it and can replace the foresail with a smaller one.

The *J24* has been used in this book to demonstrate the different techniques required to handle a larger boat. And it also features in the sections on anchoring and mooring alongside, as these techniques apply to cruisers more than dinghies.

The third type of sailing craft featured in this book is the sailboard. It is only one tenth as heavy as a *470* and one hundredth the weight of a *J24*. Sailboards are extremely fast, faster sometimes than the wind that propels them. The world speed record for a sailboard is over 44 knots!

The invention of the sailboard was the start of a revolution because for the first time it was possible to move the sail to exactly the position you wanted and at the same time to angle the hull exactly as you wanted it, too. You can do this because the mast is attached to the board by a universal joint allowing the sail to be angled in any direction. The windsurfer holds onto a wishbone-shaped boom, and by moving this he can use the force of the wind in the sail to steer the sailboard, and so a rudder is not necessary. He can also use his own weight to make the board turn.

The sailboard's rig is extremely simple and, apart from the boom, there are no controls for adjusting the amount of power in the sail. So, if the wind becomes too strong, the windsurfer has to come ashore, take off his sail, and replace it with a smaller one.

The section on windsurfing demonstrates that a sailboard uses the principles of sailing reduced to their purest forms which makes it all the more attractive to handle.

Opposite page: a *470* under way with mainsail, jib, and spinnaker hoisted. The trapeze is being used to suspend the crew well outboard. Below: This sailboard is ideal for light and medium winds because it has a retractable dagger board like a dinghy. In strong winds it is best to change to a smaller sailboard without one.

A *J24* with spinnaker up.

performance for its size and has become popular and successful internationally as a racing class.

It is simply designed without complex equipment, and in many ways it is sailed like a dinghy. However, unlike a dinghy it sails well even when heeling at a considerable angle. But, as the weight of its keel is less than usual for a cruising boat, the *J24* also relies on the weight of a crew of five to contribute to its stability. This makes it an exciting boat to sail in coastal waters, but unsuitable for cruising or racing off-shore as the combination of heavy seas and high wind would make it impossible to handle.

Knots and ropework

Above: the clove hitch is used for tying a mooring line to a post. Two clove hitches like this are tied to the shaft of a flag before hoisting it on the halyard.

There are many knots that can be used to tie the ropes on a boat. The ones illustrated here are the ones normally used and are the ones which you really do need to know how to tie. A knot that comes undone could be dangerous

To distinguish between the ropes on a yacht, sailors often give a particular rope a name which describes its use. The ropes that are pulled to haul up the sails are known as halyards. When out on the water the sails have to be continually adjusted to the wind, known as sheeting, and the ropes used to do this are called sheets. Ropes used to tie a boat to a quay or to moor up are known as mooring lines. And the ropes used to adjust the shape of the sails are known as control lines.

The round turn and two half hitches can be tied when the rope is under tension. It is used to secure a line round a ring, or eye. The line is first wound twice round or through the standing part in the same direction.

The stopper knot is used to stop the end of a sheet from running out completely. This version can be tied round either hand and has the advantage that it cannot jam.

The figure of eight knot is the traditional one used to stop sheets from running out. It is usually tied in the jib sheets although some people now use the stopper knot instead.

The sheet bend is used for tying together two ropes of different sizes. Never use the reef knot. This one is far superior.

The bowline is the most important knot to learn. It is a very safe knot, yet will never jam and can be untied easily. The method shown for tying it relies on a twist of the wrist at stage two. It is the best way of tying the bowline because you are in control of the rope all the time. With practice you will find it is quicker to tie this way.

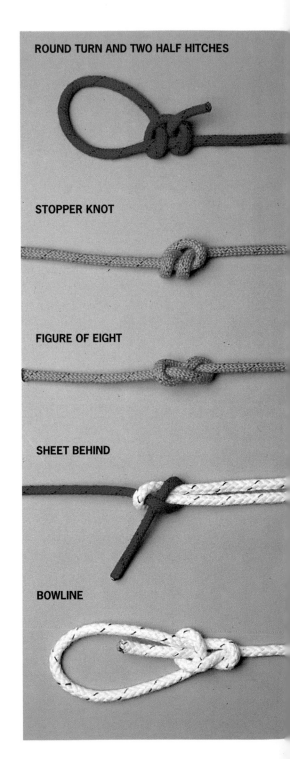

ROUND TURN AND TWO HALF HITCHES

STOPPER KNOT

FIGURE OF EIGHT

SHEET BEHIND

BOWLINE

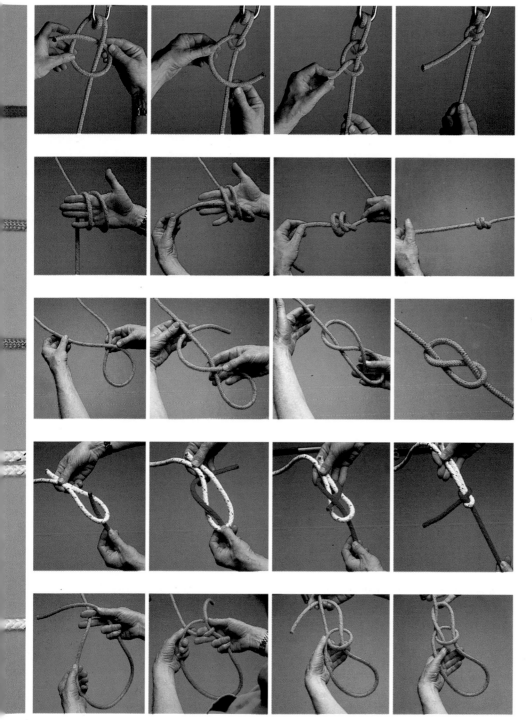

Above: when fixing a line to a cleat, you can finish with a twist to make a back hitch. Never put a back hitch on a halyard which has to be released quickly.

Above: When coiling a stranded rope give it a twist each time so that the stranding is tightened up.

Buoyancy aids and sailing clothes

Dinghy sailors wear buoyancy aids (see above and 1) in case they capsize. An adult's buoyancy aid has a flotation of about 8 kgs, and will only support someone for a short time in water. (Dinghy sailors should never leave capsized craft.) A buoyancy aid is often referred to as a lifejacket, but a lifejacket has a positive buoyancy of at least 16 kgs, and will support the head of an unconscious person face up. A buoyancy aid cannot do that.

Before buying a buoyancy aid check to see that it is the right size for the wearer. Beginners *must* wear one, or a lifejacket which, though bulky, may make them feel even more secure. Sailing clubs have strict rules about buoyancy aids. Some insist they are worn in heavy weather, while others rule that they must be carried on board, or indeed worn at all times.

Suitable clothing matters. Even on warm days the wind chill factor is significant, particularly when sailing upwind. If your clothes are wet the evaporation of water off them will cool you down. So the best clothes are the ones that water runs off rapidly and are resistant to wind.

Traditionally, warm clothes are worn beneath waterproof ones like oilskins; these are still used on larger boats. But dinghy sailors prefer to use a waterproof dinghy suit (2) or, if it is cold, a Neoprene wetsuit (3). The wetsuit traps water between the suit and the wearer. This forms extra insulation but you have to get wet before it works.

Additional protection can be obtained from a drysuit (4) which has waterproof seals and zips. This prevents the ingress of water, but condensation can be severe. Gloves are not particularly effective in keeping the hands warm, but lightweight ones (5) protect them from rope blisters. Sailing shoes, or boots (6), with proper grips are essential to stop you sliding all over the deck.

BASIC SAILING TECHNIQUES
Parts of the dinghy 1

The following four pages show the parts of the dinghy and explain their functions. A complete newcomer to sailing will soon discover that there is a new language to be mastered. The terminology, and this is defined more broadly in the glossary at the end of this book, very quickly becomes part of your sailing vocabulary and, after only a couple of outings and being practically involved with rigging the dinghy, it will soon become more familiar.

The mast (1) is supported by two shrouds (2), which are kept in position by the spreaders (3), and a forestay (4). The mast passes through the mast gate (5) down to the floor of the dinghy where it is held firmly by the heel in the mast step. The jib (6) is hoisted by the jib halyard (7). The main halyard (8) hoists the mainsail (shown on page 19) to the top of the mast. In

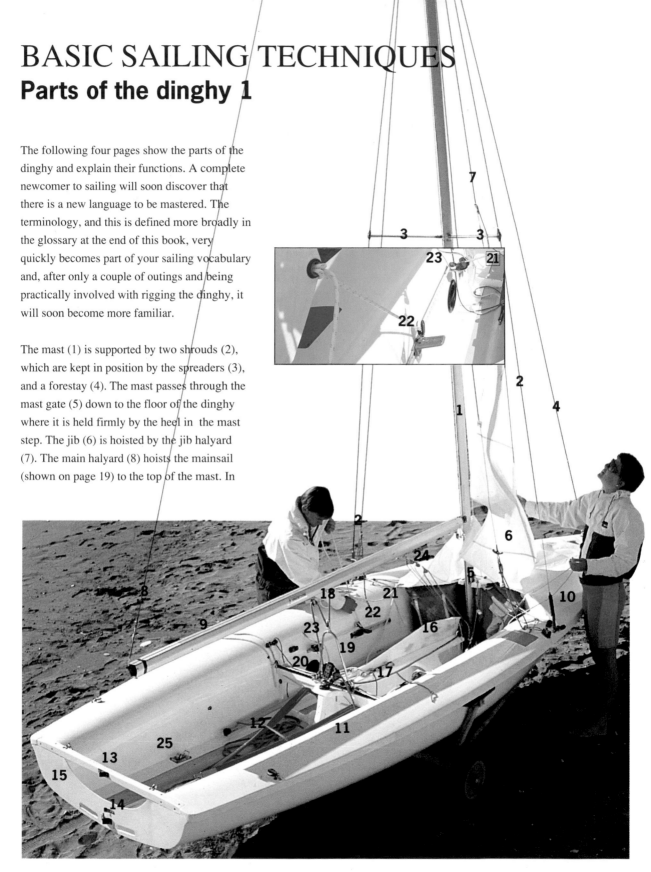

this picture the main halyard is being used to hold up the boom (9) on to which the mainsail is attached. Under the foredeck (10) and side decks (11) there are airtight buoyancy compartments. The crew put their feet under the toe straps (12) when leaning out to balance the boat. The gudgeon (13) and pintle (14) hold the rudder (shown on page 18) on the transom (15). The centreboard (16) is lowered from the centreboard casing (17) when sailing. The main sheet (18) passes through a series of pulleys. One is attached to a hoop (19) which can be pulled across the boat on the main sheet traveller (20). The main sheet and jib sheets (21) are ropes used by the crew to control the sails. Each jib sheet passes through a fairlead (22) and is then held by a jamming cleat (23) called a camcleat. In 23(a) the sheet is about to be pulled down into a camcleat and 23(b) shows how it is held by the camcleat's two moving grippers. To release the sheet you just jerk it upwards. Another type of jamming cleat 23(c) does not have any moving parts and is used to hold other ropes. When a rope is held in this way it is known as being cleated. The kicking strap (24), or vang, runs from the bottom of the mast to a point on the boom. Its function is to prevent the boom from rising excessively. The self bailer (25) removes any water which may come aboard. When open 25(a) it sucks the water out. This is done by the speed of the dinghy creating a low pressure area behind the bailer. It requires a good speed to create sufficient suction. At low speeds water will just leak in and the bailer needs to be shut by pushing down on the wire lever 25(b). When closed 25(c) the bailer presents a smooth surface to the water and is watertight. Always check the bailer is closed when mooring. On the *470* there are two self bailers.

Parts of the dinghy 2

The rudder and the centreboard are the two parts of the dinghy which control it under the water. The helmsman steers the dinghy with the rudder. The centreboard stops the dinghy from being blown sideways by the wind.

The 470 has a rudder which can be fitted to the transom before launching as its blade (1) can be raised. As soon as the boat is in deep water the blade can be lowered. The blade is kept down by pulling on its lanyard (2) which is then cleated to the tiller (3). The pin, or pintle, and gudgeon, or eye, of the rudder fit into the gudgeon and pintle on the transom so that the rudder swings freely. It is essential that you do not not lose the rudder if your boat capsizes. On the 470 there is a plastic clip (4) which prevents it falling off if the boat is inverted. The rudder is controlled by the helmsman with a hinged tiller extension (5) which allows the helmsman to steer from any position. The picture on the opposite page illustrates how the extension is used giving control at some distance.

The centreboard is raised and lowered by the ropes which pass round the centreboard

Right top: Rudder raised.
Middle: Rudder lowered.
Bottom: Rudder blade held in position by the lanyard.
Above right: the centreboard case. The centreboard pivots inside this and can be raised or lowered as shown in the diagrams (below).

case (6). Pull on one to raise it; pull on the other to lower it. It can be fully (7a) or partially (7b) lowered, or raised completely depending on the sailing conditions.

Some dinghies only have a mainsail (8) but a 470 also has a foresail which is usually called a jib (9). The parts of both sails have the same names. They are hoisted by wire halyards, one being attached to the mainsail head (10) and the other to the head of the jib (16). The luff (11) of the mainsail runs up a groove in the mast; the luff of the jib (17) is attached to the forestay wire. The foot (12) of the mainsail slides into the boom to which it is attached by the tack (13) and the clew (14); the foot of the jib (18) is free.

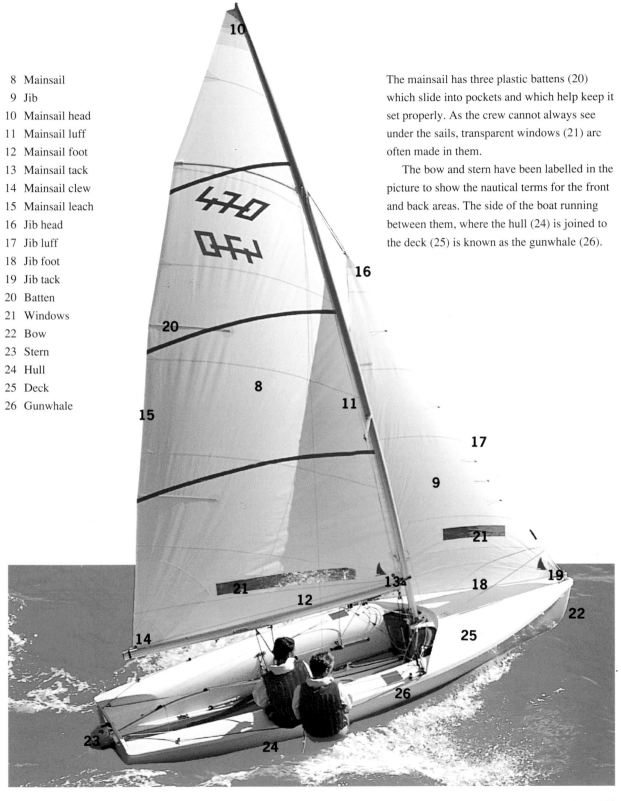

8 Mainsail
9 Jib
10 Mainsail head
11 Mainsail luff
12 Mainsail foot
13 Mainsail tack
14 Mainsail clew
15 Mainsail leach
16 Jib head
17 Jib luff
18 Jib foot
19 Jib tack
20 Batten
21 Windows
22 Bow
23 Stern
24 Hull
25 Deck
26 Gunwhale

The mainsail has three plastic battens (20) which slide into pockets and which help keep it set properly. As the crew cannot always see under the sails, transparent windows (21) arc often made in them.

The bow and stern have been labelled in the picture to show the nautical terms for the front and back areas. The side of the boat running between them, where the hull (24) is joined to the deck (25) is known as the gunwhale (26).

Basic sailing terms

DIAGRAM 1

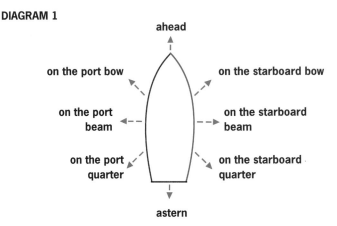

The language of sailing, particulary when defining techniques and manoevres, may seem strange, but you will quickly become accustomed to it. Sailors have to be constantly aware of the wind direction and many nautical terms relate to that as well.

Firstly, it is important to learn the phrases used to describe the direction from which the wind is blowing when you are sitting in a boat (*diagram 1*). These same phrases are also used to describe where objects like another boat, the land, or a buoy, are in relation to your boat. They remain the same whichever direction your boat is sailing. For example, if there is a buoy in front of you (ahead) and to the left (port) you say it is 'on the port bow'. The port side is the left side of the boat as you look to the bow; the right hand side is the starboard side. They have their colours, too. Port is red (which you can remember by thinking of the drink) and starboard is green. These are important when you learn about navigating a boat.

Port is always the left hand side of the boat and starboard is always the right hand side. But in *diagram 2* it can be seen that the windward and leeward sides of a boat do not remain the same. They change according to where the wind

is blowing from. The windward side of the boat is always the side from which the wind is blowing, irrespective of the direction in which the boat is sailing. Similarly, a wind blowing from the shore is called an off-shore wind and one blowing towards the shore is called an on-shore wind.

Diagram 2 also shows that when you sail as close as possible to the direction from which the wind is blowing it is described as being 'close hauled' (1 and 3), or sailing upwind, and both sails are pulled right in.

When the wind is coming from the starboard (right) side of the boat it is said to be on the 'starboard tack'; when it is blowing from the port (left) side it is on the 'port tack'.

If you want to change from one tack to another you usually turn the boat towards the direction of the wind and keep it swinging round until the wind catches the sails on the other side of the boat. This manoeuvre is called 'tacking'. In 2 the dinghy is facing directly into the wind and the sails are flapping because the wind cannot fill them. This is called being 'head to wind'. If you turn the boat away from the wind instead of towards it, the sails will eventually want to fill on the opposite side. This is known as gybing (8). Turning towards the wind, but not tacking, is called 'luffing up' (10 and 12); turning away from the wind, but not gybing, is called 'bearing away' (4 and 6).

A boat can, of course, sail in the same direction as the wind is blowing. Both sails are let right out. This is called 'running' (7 and 9), or sailing downwind.

In between close hauled and running, a boat is said to be 'reaching' (5 and 11). This is when the wind is not blowing from nearly in front (on the bow), or from behind (astern), but from the side (abeam).

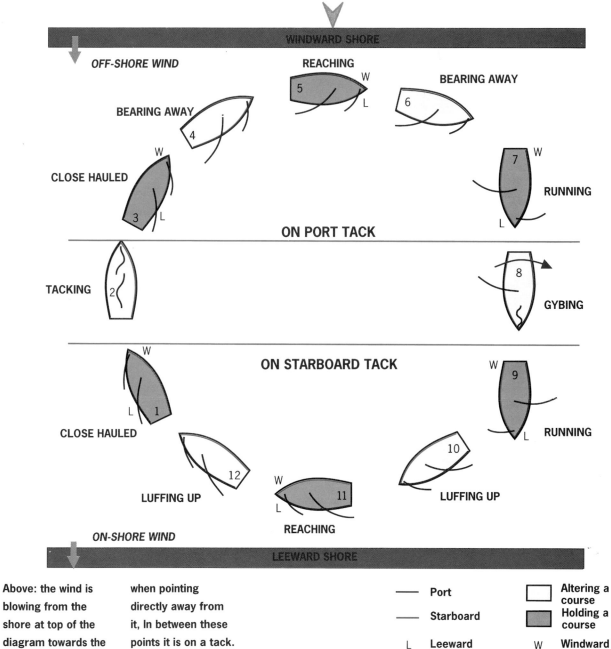

DIAGRAM 2

WINDWARD SHORE

OFF-SHORE WIND

REACHING

BEARING AWAY

BEARING AWAY

5 W
L

6

CLOSE HAULED

4

7 W

RUNNING

3 W
L

ON PORT TACK

L

TACKING

2

8

GYBING

ON STARBOARD TACK

9 W
L

RUNNING

1 W
L

CLOSE HAULED

12

LUFFING UP

10

LUFFING UP

11 W
L

ON-SHORE WIND

REACHING

LEEWARD SHORE

Above: the wind is blowing from the shore at top of the diagram towards the shore at the bottom. The boat tacks when it points directly into the wind and gybes when pointing directly away from it, In between these points it is on a tack.

When sails are set to starboard, the boat is on a port tack and vice versa.

—— Port

—— Starboard

L Leeward

☐ Altering a course

▨ Holding a course

W Windward

21

Basic sailing controls

Above and left: The helmsman steers the boat by pushing or pulling on the tiller extension which changes the angle of the rudder, and turns the boat as shown in the diagram.

Most dinghies are sailed by two people with the helmsman in command and giving instructions. The helmsman is the person who steers, and the rudder and tiller together are known as the helm. 'Taking the helm' means taking charge of the steering. The helmsman also controls the main sheet. The crew is in charge of the jib sheets, uses the trapeze and is normally the one who lowers and raises the centreboard.

It is a good idea to act as the crew for an experienced helmsman before you take the helm yourself. This will give you the 'feel' of the dinghy and how it moves and heels according to the strength of the wind.

Let us assume that you have found a companion who has been willing to take you out as crew for a few times and that you now have some idea how a dinghy responds to wind and water. Today is the day you are going to take the helm for the first time. Your companion has chosen a fine day with a gentle breeze for your first attempt. Although you can start sailing in a racing dinghy like a *470*, it is better to choose a simpler type to begin with. Your companion should find a sheltered, uncrowded stretch of water and sail the boat on a reach. Carefully change positions and sit on the side deck to windward. Take the tiller extension in one hand and the main sheet in the other. You may find the extension awkward to handle at first. But if you do not use it you will not be able sit comfortably on the side deck as is the helmsman in the picture on the left.

You must, of course, understand how the rudder works. *Diagram 1* shows that if you push the tiller extension away from you, it turns the rudder towards your side of the boat. The pressure of the water on the rudder turns the boat towards the wind (luffing up). *Diagram 2* shows that if you pull the tiller extension

DIAGRAM 1

TURN TO STARBOARD

DIAGRAM 2

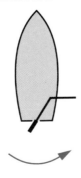

TURN TO PORT

towards you, it turns the rudder away from your side of the boat and the boat will turn away from the wind (bearing away). Practise moving the tiller extension gradually at first and see how the boat responds.

While you are experimenting with the helm you will also be holding the main sheet in your other hand. Pulling it in will bring the boom – and the mainsail – towards you. Letting it out allows the boom to swing away from you. *Diagram 3* shows how, while holding the boat on a steady course and keeping the tiller central, the main sheet controls the power of the wind in the mainsail. Letting out the main sheet fully spills the wind from the sail. There is, therefore, no longer any power in the sail and the boat ceases to heel, slows down and stops. If you now pull in the main sheet to where it was originally, this will restore the power of the wind in the mainsail and the boat starts moving and picks up speed.

Diagram 4 shows the other way of controlling the power in the sails. This is by using the rudder to luff up until the sails are only partially filled with the wind. With reduced power, the boat again ceases to heel and slows down. If you then pull the tiller towards you and bear away, the sails will fill and the boat will pick up speed again. If you had allowed the boat to luff up until it was head to wind the boat would have stopped with the sails flapping.

There is a useful way of remembering, when steering from the normal position on the windward side, which tack you are on and whether you have the right of way – other boats have to give way to you if you are on a starboard tack. Your right hand is always forwards on the starboard tack, your left hand is always forwards on the port tack. Therefore, when your right hand is forwards, you are always in the right.

Above: Choose a fine day with a gentle breeze for your first sail.

DIAGRAM 3

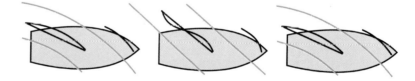

DIAGRAM 4

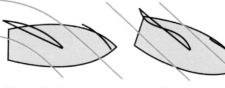
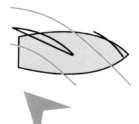
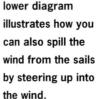

Above: the top diagram shows how you can spill the wind from the sails by letting out the main sheet. The

lower diagram illustrates how you can also spill the wind from the sails by steering up into the wind.

23

Points of sailing

On the previous page you were sailing on a reach at right angles to the wind. This is called a beam reach. But there are other points of sailing. If you luff up slightly this becomes a close reach while if you bear away from the wind you are on a broach reach. If you continue to bear away from the wind when you are on a broad reach you will start running. If you continue to luff up when on a close reach you will become close hauled. Go even closer to the wind and the luff of the sail will start to quiver. This happens when the wind starts to blow from the opposite side of the sail and is known as lifting. Continue and you will lose power, the sails will flap, and the boat will stop. This is the 'no-go' area shown in the diagram. Its angle depends on the type of boat you are sailing, but it is about 45 degrees either side of the direction of the wind.

Reaching

When the wind is abeam, you feel it on the side of your head if you are facing the bow. The sails are in a midway position. When you steer a steady course, you constantly adjust the sails to the wind and water conditions by easing out the sheets until the sail starts to lift and then pulling them in a fraction. If the boat heels excessively because of a gust of wind the sheets can be released to spill it from the sails.

Running

The wind is astern and you feel it on the back of your head when facing the bow. The sheets are let out fully. When running, the boat does not heel. The jib is being held on the opposite side to the mainsail to catch the free wind, and this is known as goose-winging.

Do not allow the boat to turn any further away from the wind or the wind will get behind the mainsail. This is called sailing 'by the lee' which is dangerous because if too much wind gets behind the mainsail the boom will whip across unexpectedly. This is called an involuntary gybe and it can damage the rigging, or even cause a capsize. How to perform a controlled gybe is explained later.

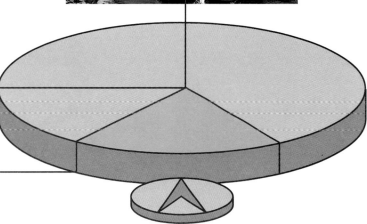

WIND DIRECTION

Close hauled

The wind is on the bow and you feel it on your face if you are facing the bow. The sheets are pulled hard in. The helmsman adjusts his course so that he can sail as close as possible to the wind without entering the no-go area shown in the diagram. If the boat heels excessively the helmsman can either let out his main sheet or luff up into the wind.

The diagram above shows the points of sailing and the 'no-go' area. The wind direction is shown by the blue arrow and it will be used throughout the book.

Hoisting the sails

Before you hoist the sails the boat should be facing head to wind to prevent the sails filling before you are ready. You should also always look up the full length of the mast and check that the halyards are able to run freely before you attach them to the sails.

The equipment and methods described and shown in these sequences are typical of the modern racing dinghy.

Below: hoisting the sails of the dinghy ready for launching.

Jib: shackle the tack to the bow. The sheets are passed through the fairleads on each side of the boat. Put a figure-of-eight knot into the end of each sheet to avoid them being pulled back through the fairleads. The halyard is shackled on to the head. The sail can now be hoisted, and the halyard tensioned and secured. On the *470* a system of pulleys allows adjustment from the centre of the boat.

Shackle jib to bow

Thread jib sheets

Figure of eight knot

Shackle halyard to head

Hoist the sail

Connect halyard to tensioner

Mainsail: slide the clew of the mainsail into and along the groove to the aft end of the boom until the outhaul wire, which adjusts the tension in the foot of the sail, can be shackled to it. The tack is fixed to the boom by a pin. The battens are inserted. Shackle the halyard on to the head. Slide it into the groove of the mast. Hoist the sail. On the *470* the halyard is secured by hooking its looped end over a rack on the mast.

The boom is then attached to the gooseneck – the hinged pivot which allows the boom to swing freely on the mast. Finally, a line is passed through an eye in the sail, known as the Cunningham hole. This line is used to tension the luff of the mainsail. The use of control lines like the outhaul and the Cunningham, which are used to control the shape of the mainsail, is explained later.

Insert clew into boom groove

Shackle outhaul to clew

Insert battens

Shackle halyard to head

Insert head into mast groove

Hoist the sail

Loop halyard over rack

Insert boom into gooseneck

Thread Cunningham line

Launching and beaching in off-shore wind

1

2

1B

With an off-shore wind, launching and beaching are relatively simple, but it is important to keep the bow of the dinghy facing into the wind when these manoeuvres are carried out. If the dinghy is placed side on to the wind while launching it may well topple off its trolley after the sails have been hoisted; and if you try and hold the boat facing away from the wind when its in the water it will probably sail off without you! When beaching, the main problem is to judge when to stop. If in doubt, it pays to stop early, as you can always get under way again and have another try.

2B

3B

3   **4**   **5**

Launching (above):

1 Lift the front of the launching trolley and push the boat stern first into the water. The rudder blade is fully raised so that it cannot hit the bottom when you lift.

2 Keep pushing until the boat floats. If you haven't already done it, now is the last time to check that you remembered to close the self bailers.

3 As the boat floats off, pull the launching trolley out of the water. The helmsman holds the boat by the bow while the crew takes the trolley out of the water and parks it safely.

4 The helmsman partly drops the rudder blade to give him a degree of steering control while still ensuring it will not hit the bottom. The crew climbs into the boat while the helmsman holds the stern. As the boat is no longer being held by the bow it begins to swing away from the wind.

5 Because the boat has swung away from the wind the sails fill and the boat will start to move away from the shore. The helmsman can help the boat on its way by giving it a push to get it into sufficiently deep water before stepping in.

Beaching (left):

1B The crew raises the centreboard as the helmsman steers into the wind and takes the speed off the boat.

2B The crew steps out of the boat.

3B The crew holds the boat with its bow into the wind while the helmsman raises the rudder. Pull the boat out of the water using the trolley.

Before you sail, it is important to check that the boat has been rigged correctly. You do not want to find that there is a problem when you are drifting away from the shore and unable to get back again. And, before you finally decide on where to launch, you must always think about getting back.

A boat that is disabled will drift downwind. So, though it may be easy to launch and beach from a windward shore, it is hard to get back to it. In contrast, it is harder to launch into an on-shore wind, but if something does go wrong, it is easier to get back.

Launching and beaching in on-shore or cross-shore wind

Launching and beaching with an on-shore or a cross-shore breeze is more difficult than with an off-shore wind because the wind is either behind the boat as it is being launched or beached, or sideways to it. An on-shore breeze blows directly onto the beach while a cross-shore breeze is roughly parallel to it.

Launching: with the wind on-shore it is possible to launch the dinghy bow first or stern first. But if you launch it bow first you will have to float it over the front of the trolley which can cause problems unless you have a proper slipway. It is therefore important to learn how to launch it stern first even though the boat is not head to wind. This is not a problem with the jib because it can be allowed to flap by letting the sheets right out. But if the mainsail is hoisted it is not possible to spill all the wind from it and the boat will become uncontrollable. Therefore, it is essential that the boat is launched from its trolley before the mainsail is fully hoisted (*picture below left*).

Once in the water the crew holds the bow of the boat and the stern will be swung round by the wind. The crew must stand in sufficiently deep water to allow the boat to swing right round until its bow is head to wind. The boat is now stable and the helmsman can climb aboard and hoist the mainsail (*picture below centre*).

As the boat is going to have to sail close hauled to leave the shore, the helmsman chooses which tack he wants to sail on. He tells the crew who pulls the boat towards her until she can grasp its side (*picture below right*). She then manoeuvres the boat until it is pointing in the right direction, and gives it a push before climbing aboard. It is important that the helmsman partly lowers the centreboard which will help prevent the boat being blown sideways when it starts moving. It should be fully lowered as soon as the depth of water allows.

Beaching: in the sequence of photographs on the right the boat is being beached in a cross-shore breeze. When approaching the shore to beach it is essential to put the boat head to wind while you still have plenty of room to manoeuvre. The mainsail should then be lowered, the centreboard raised, and the boat can then be steered to the shore under the power of the jib alone.

1

Below left: the sequence shows the boat being held in the water while the mainsail is raised.

The diagram and illustrations above and right show: 1 heading toward shore under full sail; 2 heading into the wind and lowering mainsail; 3 steering back toward shore using jib. In the pictures far right and near right the sequence is completed.

31

Sitting correctly

Above left: the helmsman and crew are sitting too far apart. Above opposite: they are sitting correctly together.

Where you sit in a dinghy is very important as the weight of both you and your crew can have a marked effect on performance. To achieve maximum speed with your dinghy it is important that you keep it as upright as possible because heeling reduces the efficiency of both sails and centreboard. When the boat starts heeling, sit on the windward side deck. If it heels more, lean out and balance yourself by putting your feet under the toe straps, and your crew should do the same.

If you sit apart, you present two obstructions to the wind. This adversely effects the flow of wind, particularly when close hauled. Also, if you sit apart in stronger winds, when waves are present, the boat tends to bash into them instead of climbing over them. To ensure the smoothest ride, the bow and stern of the dinghy should have as little weight in them

as possible. So sit together in the middle where the movement is least.

When the boat is running you and your crew should sit on opposite sides of the boat as this helps its stability.

In very light winds you also sit on opposite sides when reaching or running as the crew should sit to leeward to counterbalance the weight of the helmsman. When there is insufficient wind to fill the sails the crew heels the boat slightly to leeward. This action allows both of the sails to take up the correct curvature because of their own weight, and enables them to take the fullest advantage of even the least puff of wind.

In light winds you sit forward. Only move aft when you start planing, which is when the boat rises out of the water and rides on its bow wave. This is covered later.

Far left: the helmsman is sitting correctly for light wind sailing as the transom is nearly out of the water. Near left: you can tell from the increased wash that the transom is too deep in the water because the helmsman is sitting too far aft.

Running, reaching, and close hauled

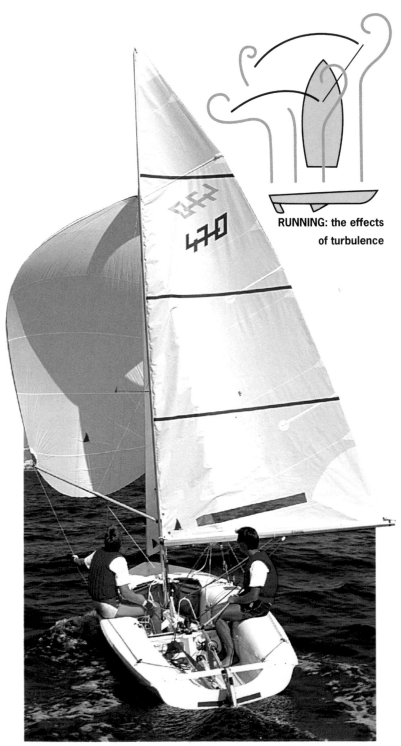

RUNNING: the effects of turbulence

Running: when a dinghy is running, the wind is blowing directly from astern. The main sheet has been let out until the mainsail can go no further. The boat is not heeling. The spinnaker can be used when the boat is running to increase the boat's speed. It is also used on a broad reach but rarely on a close reach unless the wind is light. Handling the spinnaker is explained later, but notice that when it is hoisted the helmsman swaps places with the crew and moves to the leeward side. This allows the crew to have a good view for trimming the spinnaker. The centreboard has been raised so that only a small portion remains in the water to aid stability. In the diagram (*top left*) you can see that the wind, because it is faster than the boat, is flowing past it and swirling in front of the sails. This is called turbulence.

Reaching: this is the fastest point of sailing. The centreboard is usually partly retracted. Helmsman and crew are using their weight to prevent the boat from heeling excessively. To do this on the *470* the crew uses a trapeze harness. This is clipped to a wire attached to the mast and suspends the whole body away from the boat. Trapeze techniques are explained later.

Here, the wind is abeam so the sails are pulled about halfway in from the running position, but they need to be constantly trimmed, as it is called, to respond to any variations in the wind.

The airflow diagram (*above right*) shows that the wind is flowing smoothly and that there is no longer any turbulence. The wind is deflected by the sails and creates a force approximately at right angles to them. This force drives the boat forwards and it also causes the boat to heel. How this force is created is explained later.

REACHING: airflow

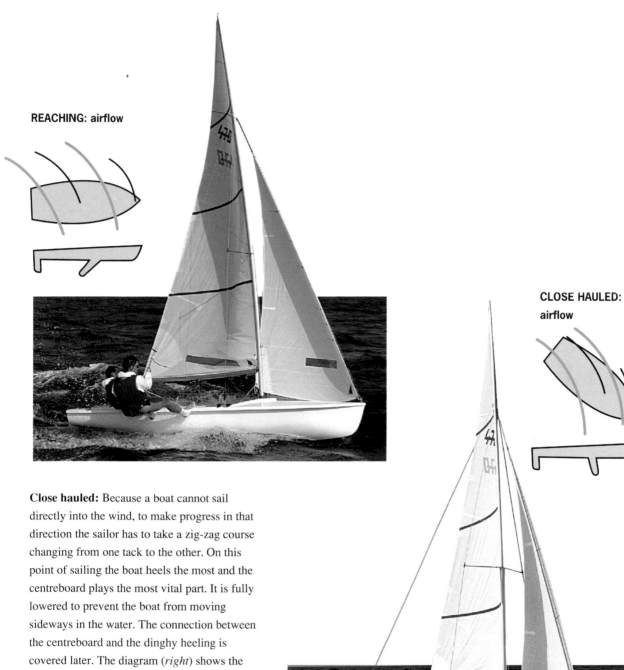

CLOSE HAULED: airflow

Close hauled: Because a boat cannot sail directly into the wind, to make progress in that direction the sailor has to take a zig-zag course changing from one tack to the other. On this point of sailing the boat heels the most and the centreboard plays the most vital part. It is fully lowered to prevent the boat from moving sideways in the water. The connection between the centreboard and the dinghy heeling is covered later. The diagram (*right*) shows the wind is flowing smoothly. But, compared with reaching, more of the force created by the sails deflecting the wind is directed towards heeling and less towards driving the boat forward. The sails are pulled in close to the centre line which is why it is called close hauled.

Great skill is required to keep the boat on a course which is as finely angled to the wind as possible without losing too much speed.

Tacking

Tacking is passing from one tack to another through the 'eye' of the wind and is also known as 'going about'. The centreboard is fully lowered. Look to make sure you have room to manoeuvre, and remember to duck when the boom swings over. Steady pressure on the tiller is best. This increases the angle of the rudder gradually which encourages the boat to turn quickly. Keep the rudder turned until the tack is almost completed and only then straighten it up gradually.

Tack only when you have sufficient speed. If you are sailing fast enough it is possible to tack from one reach to another, but normally you only tack when close hauled. Unless you have sufficient boat speed you will not have the impetus to complete the turn. If this happens you will be stuck head to wind, 'in stays' as it is called, and your boat will stop. To start sailing again you have to put the tiller hard over to one side and your crew pulls the jib over to the other side until it fills with wind. This is known as 'backing' the jib. It pushes the boat's bow away from the wind so that you can start sailing again – not a very elegant manoeuvre!

Always alert your crew before tacking by giving the clear command '**Ready about**'. Both of you then remove the main and jib sheets from their jamming cleats. As you start pushing the tiller extension away from you to bring the boat into the wind you give the command '**Lee-oh**' (*picture 1*). Your crew now lets out the jib sheets a little. This helps the boat luff up into the wind (*picture 2*), but the jib sheet is not released completely until the jib is 'aback', that is when the wind begins to fill the other side of it. Holding the the jib aback helps the boat turn more quickly. It also makes for a neater tack and prevents the jib from

flapping. As the boat passes through the eye of the wind both you and your crew should change sides together. Do this as smoothly as possible. Any violent movements will effect your boat's speed (*picture 3*).

Because the *470* has a centre main sheet, you face forwards as you change sides. You hold the sheet in one hand and the tiller extension in the other, and then flip the extension behind your back (*picture 4*). As you cross you swap hands by momentarily holding the main sheet in your tiller hand.

Ease the main sheet after the boat has passed through the eye of the wind. This helps the boat bear away. As the boat accelerates pull the sheet in gradually and your crew should do

the same. It is a common error to pull the jib in too quickly. The boat is now sailing normally on the opposite tack (*picture 5*).

In this demonstration our sailors have kept the boat reasonably level so that you can see what is happening inside the boat. If they were racing, they would use the tactic of rolling the boat to help it to turn and to give a boost to the wind in the sails.

3

Above left: the boom swings across the boat when tacking so remember to duck.

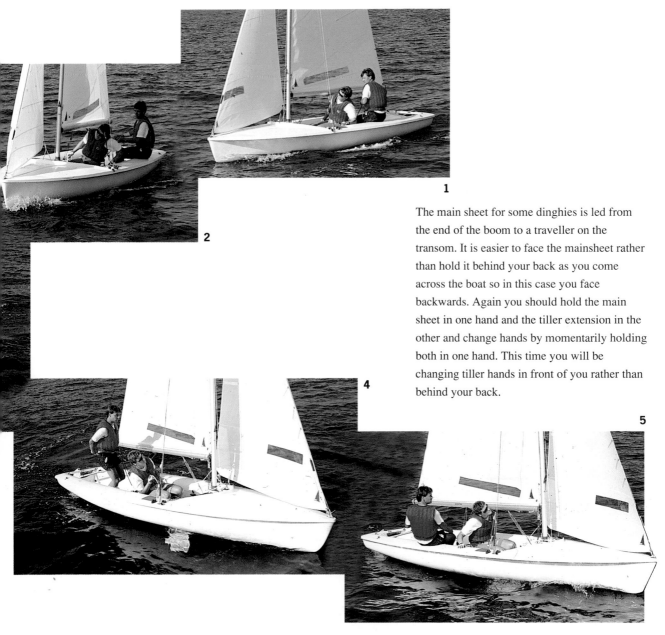

1

2

4

5

The main sheet for some dinghies is led from the end of the boom to a traveller on the transom. It is easier to face the mainsheet rather than hold it behind your back as you come across the boat so in this case you face backwards. Again you should hold the main sheet in one hand and the tiller extension in the other and change hands by momentarily holding both in one hand. This time you will be changing tiller hands in front of you rather than behind your back.

Gybing

2

3

4

6

5

1

across (4) and then you move to the other side of the boat (5). The boat is still turning.

Allow the main sheet to run right out on the new tack as this prevents the boat luffing up sharply. Make sure the boom does not bang against the shrouds (6). Then change hands on the tiller and trim the sheets to their correct positions for your new course.

Gybing can be risky in strong winds, and unless you have confidence in your boat and your ability to handle it you may feel safer, to start with at any rate, to take the long way round and tack instead – a manoeuvre which is known as 'wearing round'.

If you do decide to gybe in a strong wind do not slow down. As you are sailing away from the wind the weight of it decreases the faster you go. Try and gybe just after a gust as your boat speed will still be high but the wind will be temporarily reduced. Raising the centreboard will reduce the amount the boat heels after the gybe.

In light winds it is not essential to pull the sail over, but in strong wings it is vital to do so. Do not wait for the wind to slam it over as serious damage can result. If your timing is good the boom will gently come across the boat under control and without a huge weight of wind in the sail.

If the mainsail comes across rapidly, when it reaches the end of its swing the boat will tend to luff up sharply. You should anticipate this by taking corrective action with the rudder.

Finally, the crew should be ready to move quickly to sit out on the new tack, particularly as the rounding up action will cause the dinghy to heel. If you do not take corrective action sufficiently quickly, the boat will luff up into the wind so violently that you could have a capsize on your hands.

Gybing is the opposite to tacking, in that you change tack by turning away from the eye of the wind. When this happens the boom will pass over the boat rapidly as the wind switches to the other side of the mainsail. Because of this, gybing has to be carefully controlled. Normally when gybing, the centreboard is partially raised.

Unlike tacking, boat speed is unnecessary for gybing as the mainsail will be driving the boat throughout the manoeuvre.

Before gybing, check that the main sheet is free to run right out and is not caught in anything. Uncleat it, warn your crew you are about to gybe, then give the command '**gybe-oh**' and pull the tiller towards you (1).

As the boat starts to bear away from the wind, the jib will blow across, so your crew uncleats the sheet and holds it. You flip the tiller extension over (2).

Grabbing the parts of the main sheet immediately above the hoop, you pull the sail across. This is done to get the boom across the boat before too much wind has built up in the sail (3). Both of you duck as the boom comes

Controlling speed and heaving to

1 Lay the boat across the wind.

2 Pull the jib across.

3 Cleat the jib sheet so that the jib stays to windward.

4 The boat has now stopped. Note the absence of any wash.

You can stop by letting the wind out of the sails, either by releasing the sheets or by putting the boat head to wind. If you want to slow down but not stop, just use one sail. Then it is normally best to sail with the jib and allow the mainsail to flap. Because the mainsail is supported by the mast and boom it will flap gently. The jib, however, can flap quite violently. Not only is this noisy and unpleasant but it will damage the sail.

If you wish to sail with the mainsail alone it is best to lower the jib. This will improve your visibility, too. It is not practicable to sail any distance under the jib alone because, without the mainsail, the boat cannot make progress to windward.

Releasing the sheets or heading into the wind are perfectly acceptable ways of stopping for a short time. But if you want to stop for longer it is better to 'heave to'. To do this you lay the boat across the wind as if you were reaching and sheet the mainsail normally (*picture 1*). The crew reaches forwards and pulls the jib sheet across (*picture 2*) which is then cleated so that the jib is on the windward side (*picture 3*). When the boat has stopped, the tiller is pushed to leeward (*picture 4*) and tied if necessary. The sails do not flap and as they are acting against one another the boat drifts only slowly to leeward. If the boat does try to sail forwards, the rudder will make it turn towards the wind and stop. Then the jib will blow it back again.

Right: a dinghy being stopped by holding out the mainsail against the wind to make it act like a brake. This tactic can also be used to manoeuvre a dinghy in tight situations.

Capsizing

Any dinghy is liable to capsize. As it is bound to happen to you sooner or later, it is a good idea to practise what to do.

Remember it is always much safer to stay with your boat. If you become separated from it, swim back to it quickly.

A capsize is likely to occur when conditions are difficult and unpleasant, in high winds or rough seas, so you must know exactly what the procedure is beforehand. The time to learn what to do is on a warm day with little or no wind. Capsize your dinghy deliberately as these experts have done in this series of pictures. The boat, being upside down, is in the most difficult position to right. However, most boats will often only capsize on to their sides, in which

Above: the crew, with trapeze harness attached, has fallen overboard. In this situation a capsize often follows.

Safety first

Be confident of your ability to swim in deep water. Always wear a buoyancy aid. Practise swimming out from under the mainsail. Practise lowering the mainsail when the boat is on its side. Practise climbing back on board. Stay close to the boat at all times when in the water. Make sure that all your equipment is attached to you or the boat.

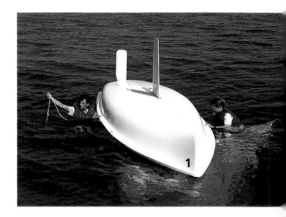

case just follow the sequence from *picture 5*.

A jib sheet is thrown across the boat (1). The helmsman joins the crew and both climb on to the gunwhale. One pulls on the jib sheet while the other pulls on the centreboard (2). They bounce on the gunwhale and this starts the boat moving (3). As the boat begins to come on to its side the crew climbs on to the centreboard. The first half of the manoeuvre is completed when the boat is lying on its side (4). (If you cannot get the boat on to its side, the only option is to wait for the rescue boat to come and right the boat.) The helmsman swims to the bow so that he can hold it pointing into the wind (5). The crew continues to stand on the centreboard and leans outwards until the dinghy begins to right

itself. If it does not, they will have to lower the mainsail. As the boat comes upright the crew climbs aboard from the centreboard (7). The boat is now upright. If the dinghy does not have much buoyancy the crew must bail out before the helmsman can climb aboard (8).

Different boats have different characteristics and you should experiment with your own. The *470*, having a very high buoyancy, floats high in the water. This makes it difficult to climb aboard over the side decks as the boat comes upright, but not much water comes aboard and it drains out easily.

Crew overboard

If you are the 'man overboard', remain calm, tread water, and watch your boat so you are ready to be picked up.

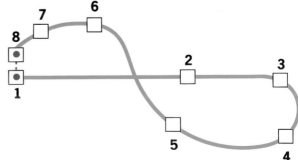

1 Crew falls overboard.
2 Helmsman sails on.
3 He judges the distance and starts to tack.
4 He tacks.
5 He bears away.
6 He judges when to turn into the wind.
7 He turns into the wind.
8 He is alongside the crew head to wind.

A common cause of man overboard is when you or your crew misses the toe straps because the boat heels unexpectedly, or when the straps break. In this picture sequence a practice drill is being carried out.

If your crew goes overboard, the immediate problem you are faced with is one of stability. Let go the sheets immediately, jib as well as main, so the boat comes upright and you can assess the situation. Make sure you know where your crew is in the water, then start sailing again on a reach. Keep your crew in sight at all times as he will drift down wind. You must tack to get back to him, but if you try and do this too quickly you will sail past him and will have to try again. Only tack when you judge you have sufficient room to turn and make the loop necessary (*see diagram*) to bring the boat alongside him. Once you have tacked you must bear away and sail downwind to leeward of your crew so that you can then bring the boat head to wind in order to stop alongside him. A quicker method of getting back to your crew is to gybe, but this is only recommended in very light weather. In stronger winds you risk a capsize because you are making the manoeuvre single-handed.

Pick up your crew from the windward side. If you lean out to leeward the weight of the sail tends to tip the boat over further, rather than helping to balance it. Help your crew aboard by lifting under his shoulders.

If the helmsman goes over the side, the crew takes the helm and performs the rescue.

The man overboard drill must be practised particularly by the crew until it is perfected. It is much harder to judge when to tack, and to return in one tack, than might be thought. Practise it in fine weather by dropping and picking up a spare buoyancy aid.

45

UNDERSTANDING WIND AND WATER
Wind force

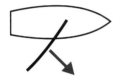

Above: when reaching, most of the force in the sail is directed to driving the boat forwards.

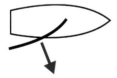

Above: when sailing close hauled most of the force in the sail is directed towards making the boat heel.

You have now learnt the rudiments of sailing as well as how to launch and beach your dinghy, and to sail in safety. But to progress from this point you must understand how the wind and water interact with your boat. The following pages show you how they do this and suggest some experiments you can make to discover how your boat responds to them. It is important that you are able to sail in sympathy with the natural forces on your boat rather than against them.

The wind creates a force which drives the boat forward and also causes it to heel - the amount of heel being dependent on the course being sailed. This is shown in the diagram (*top left*) where, on a reaching course, the arrow points more forwards than sideways, so that most of the energy is directed towards driving the boat. On a close hauled course (*bottom left*) the force acts more sideways than forwards, so most of the energy is directed towards heeling the boat.

To understand how this force is created it is necessary to consider the flow of the wind, or airflow, illustrated on page opposite by means of streamlines. The streamlines follow the shape of the sail, and note that they start to do this before they reach it. This is known as the upwash and means that the airflow is parallel to the sail as soon as it reaches it, which is why it is technically more correct to say that the wind is deflected by the sail, and not that it is filling it. As the wind passes along the sail, the air on the leeward side has to follow a longer path than the air on the windward side. Because of this it has to travel faster in order to reach the leech of the sail at the same time as the wind on the windward side. This is shown on the diagram by the streamlines. The closer they are to each other the faster the air is travelling.

The slower the airflow the greater the pressure. It follows that the pressure on the windward side is greater than the pressure on the leeward side. It is the difference between these two pressures which creates the force in the sail. The arrows in the picture on the right are a representation of these pressure differences. The greater the pressure difference the larger the arrow. The increasing curve in the sail creates an increasing difference in pressure. The sail has its maximum curvature towards the luff so that is where the maximum pressure difference occurs. The sum of all the pressures acting over the entire sail makes up the total force acting on it which throughout this book is called the wind force.

Keeping the air flowing freely over both sides of the sail maximises the power you can extract from the wind. If the airflow becomes turbulent the pressure differences are lost. For example, when a boat is running with the wind behind it, there is a greater pressure on the windward side of the sail. But, because of the turbulence in front of the sail (see diagram on page 34), the pressure there is not reduced. Therefore, the pressure differences are less and so is the wind force in the sail. This is the reason why a boat cannot travel as fast with the wind directly behind it.

Right: the arrows superimposed on this picture are a representation of the pressure differences acting all over the sail. The sum of them is called the wind force.

Above: the diagram shows the streamlines of the airflow as it meets and passes the sail.

The centreboard

Here is an experiment for you to try, which shows that the force of the wind on the sails has to be resisted by the force of the water on the centreboard. Try it out in fine weather and with plenty of room to manoeuvre.

A dinghy cannot sail to windward with its centreboard up. If it is not lowered the wind force will make it drift off to leeward as the hull alone presents little resistance to the water. Because the centreboard has a large area when it is lowered, the water pressure on it helps the boat resist the sideways push of the wind force and the boat is able to make progress in a windward direction. Without this water pressure on the centreboard or lateral resistance, as it is called, the boat will move in the direction of the wind. The sails will then have less air flowing across them and the wind force will be reduced.

The sideways push of the wind force, combined with the pressure of water on the centreboard, causes a tendency for the boat to heel. This is countered by the crew weight.

The pictures on the near right show the experiment under way: the *left hand* one shows the dinghy close hauled with the centre board lowered and with plenty of wind force in the sails. The heeling increases as the crew leans in to raise the centreboard (below).

In the *centre* picture the centreboard has been raised. Both crew and helmsman are in more or less the same position, yet the boat has come upright, showing that the tendency to heel has been almost eliminated. The bow wave has disappeared on the windward side as the speed is reduced and the boat begins to move sideways as well as forwards.

In the *right hand* pictures the boat has lost all perceptible forward movement and is moving mostly sideways with little wind force in the sails.

The wind force on the sail (blue arrow) and the water pushing the centreboard create lateral resistance (red arrow). This creates a tendency to heel which is counter-balanced by the weight of the crew and helmsman (green arrow).

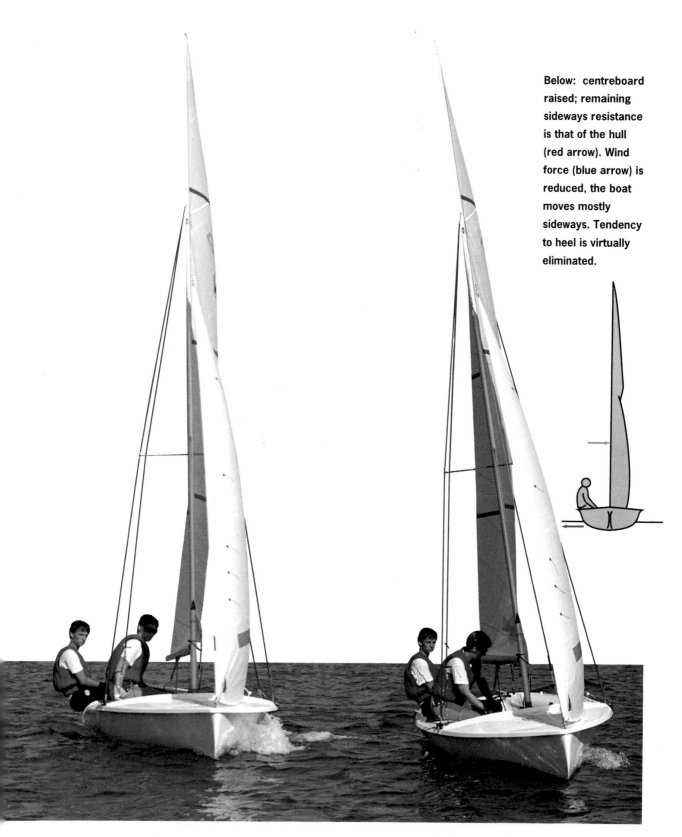

Below: centreboard raised; remaining sideways resistance is that of the hull (red arrow). Wind force (blue arrow) is reduced, the boat moves mostly sideways. Tendency to heel is virtually eliminated.

Leeway

Even with the centreboard down a boat does have some sideways motion. This is called leeway and is at its most pronounced when the boat is close hauled and then it declines as you bear away from the wind. There is no leeway when running which is why you do not need the centreboard then. Leeway also depends on the condition of the sea. In calm water it is less than 10 degrees, but it becomes much greater in rough weather due to the pounding of the waves. The centreboard resists leeway but it never eliminates it completely.

So, when sailing close hauled, the boat moves sideways as well as forwards, just as a crab does. The pictures *below* show this. Under the water the centreboard is pressed firmly against the water on its leeward side by the wind force in the sails. But on the windward side of the centreboard the crabwise motion of the boat creates a low pressure area. Just as the pressure differences in the sails create the wind force, so do the differences of water pressure on the centreboard create the lateral resistance referred to on the previous page. But it is important to note that, unlike wind force, the difference of water pressure on the centreboard only occurs because the boat is making leeway.

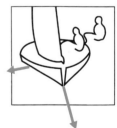

Above and left: when sailing close hauled the boat moves sideways as well as forwards. This is called leeway.

Although the keen helmsman may want to reduce this leeway it has to be present to a certain degree to provide lateral resistance. The faster your centreboard passes through the water the greater this resistance, so it is important to keep your speed up particularly when sailing through waves. If you lose speed, your leeway becomes excessive because the lateral resistance has been reduced.

If you watch a large boat from astern as it sails off on a new tack or from a mooring, you will notice that it drifts sharply to leeward until its keel has generated sufficient resistance. Remember this when you leave a mooring in a crowded anchorage. Allow enough room for your boat to move sideways until it has picked up sufficient speed.

The resistance generated by the centreboard also depends on the area of the board in the water. The greater the area the greater the resistance. So when the boat is sailing close hauled – that is when leeway is at its most pronounced – the board is always lowered fully. It is particularly important to minimise leeway when close hauled because your boat is being pushed to leeward just when you are trying to make progress in the windward direction.

Above and right: if the helmsman is heading for a mark on-shore, he will have to point well upwind of it to compensate for leeway.

Balancing the forces

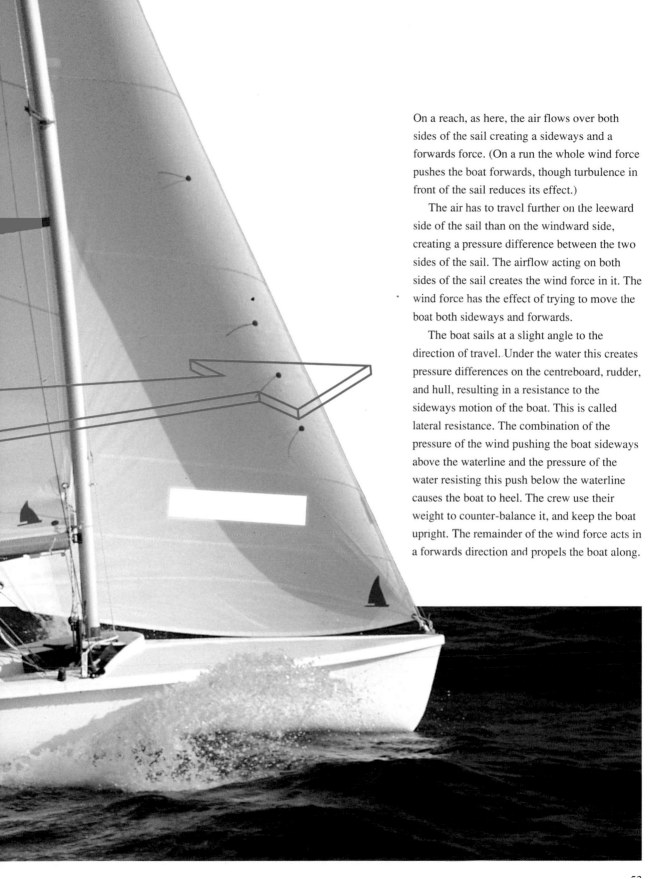

On a reach, as here, the air flows over both sides of the sail creating a sideways and a forwards force. (On a run the whole wind force pushes the boat forwards, though turbulence in front of the sail reduces its effect.)

The air has to travel further on the leeward side of the sail than on the windward side, creating a pressure difference between the two sides of the sail. The airflow acting on both sides of the sail creates the wind force in it. The wind force has the effect of trying to move the boat both sideways and forwards.

The boat sails at a slight angle to the direction of travel. Under the water this creates pressure differences on the centreboard, rudder, and hull, resulting in a resistance to the sideways motion of the boat. This is called lateral resistance. The combination of the pressure of the wind pushing the boat sideways above the waterline and the pressure of the water resisting this push below the waterline causes the boat to heel. The crew use their weight to counter-balance it, and keep the boat upright. The remainder of the wind force acts in a forwards direction and propels the boat along.

Trimming the sails: their angle to the wind

There are only two ways to adjust the angle of the sail. The first is through using the rudder to steer the boat on a different course, that is either luffing up towards the wind or bearing away from it. The other is to trim the sheets to alter the angle of the sails to the boat itself.

We have seen that efficient sailing relies on keeping the air flowing smoothly on both sides of the sails. The problem is that air will not flow round sharp curves without inducing turbulence. So the bending of the airflow should be gradual. If the sails are not pulled in far enough the airflow cannot follow the sharp curve at the luff, and turbulence is created at the luff (*diagram 1*). If the sails are pulled in too far

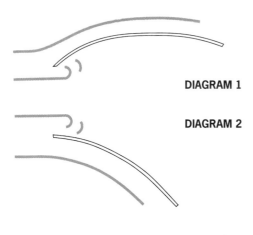

DIAGRAM 1

DIAGRAM 2

the airflow cannot follow such a sharp curve on the outside, and so turbulence sets in at the curve (*diagram 2*).

It is most important that the angles of the sails are correct where the airflow first meets them. It is also important that the air flows smoothly off the leech of the sails.

Sailing to windward:
1 The helmsman must keep the telltales flowing.
2 The windward telltales are rising, so the helmsman must bear away.
3 The leeward telltales are drooping, so the helmsman must luff up.
Right: the mainsail streamers are flowing correctly.

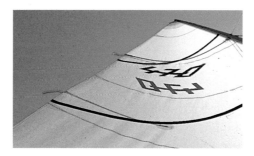

Left: the telltales on the jib are flowing correctly.

To help the helmsman keep the correct angle of the sails to the wind telltales are fitted on them which indicate the smoothness of the airflow. Both sails work together as one system so wool telltales are fitted at the luff of the jib while streamers, strips of light sailcloth, are fitted to the leech of the mainsail. On a dinghy with just one sail both telltales and streamers are fitted to it.

When there are two sails, it is the telltales on the jib which are of primary importance. These are fitted a short distance back from the luff on both sides of the sail. As long as they stream horizontally the airflow is being deflected properly. If one starts to lift or droop, this indicates that turbulence is setting in.

When sailing to windward the sheets are usually cleated and the helmsman controls the angle of the sails by altering course. He watches the jib telltales very carefully to ensure they are flowing correctly as illustrated. On a reach it is the task of the crew to adjust the trim of the jib to keep the telltales flying correctly. If the leeward ones lift, he lets the jib out. If the windward ones lift he pulls it in.

On the mainsail, it is more important to ensure that the air is flowing smoothly from the leech. The objective is to keep each streamer flying straight. Turbulence will cause them to curl, and the helmsman then takes action.

Trimming the sails: airflow through the slot

DIAGRAM 1
Flow of air through
the slot.

→ **AIRFLOW**
— **SLOT**

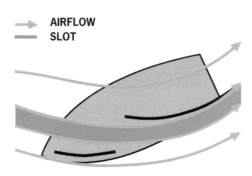

The importance of maintaining a smooth airflow over the luff of the jib and the leech of the mainsail has already been explained. But it is also important to maintain a smooth airflow in between the two sails. This gap, between the windward side of the jib and the leeward side of the mainsail, is known as the slot.

Understanding the effect of the slot is important because the wind blowing through it affects the efficiency of both sails in three ways:

1 It directs more of the airflow round the leeward side of the jib where the low pressure area is created. This is a very effective way of increasing the wind force in the jib. Some of the airflow over the mainsail is lost but the overall effect is an improvement.

2 As the jib is set in the upwash from the mainsail, the wind approaches it at a more beneficial angle than the mainsail.

Left: the crew must not obstruct the airflow through the slot.

DIAGRAM 2

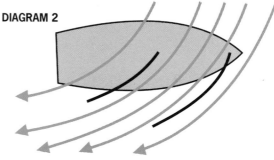

3 The air flowing through the slot is encouraged to follow the curve on the leeward side of the mainsail which in turn reduces the turbulence.

It is, therefore, very important that the slot is set up correctly. The jib should not be trimmed too tightly nor the main too loosely. *Pictures on the opposite page* illustrate well how the slot looks both from deck level and from above when both of the sails have been properly trimmed.

The effect of the slot between the jib and mainsail is diminished as the boat bears away from the wind. However, once the wind is abeam, it is possible to hoist the spinnaker (*pictures above and left*). On a reach, the airflow through the slot is then between the mainsail and the spinnaker. As with the other sails, it is very important that the spinnaker is trimmed correctly to allow the air to flow freely (*diagram 2*).

Apparent wind 1

Apparent wind is the combination of the natural wind and the wind created by the motion of the boat. It is what you feel on your face or back of your neck as you sail.

The apparent wind is important because it is also the wind which creates the wind force in the sails. So these have to be trimmed to it and not to the natural wind.

You may be feeling really warm as your boat sails downwind with just a gentle breeze playing on your back. But if you feel inclined to strip off a layer or two of clothing remember to prepare yourself for when the boat starts sailing upwind, because suddenly it will seem a much

Right: The dinghy is sailing towards the wind. Its own speed increases the apparent wind.

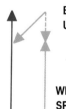

DIAGRAM 2

BOAT SPEED
UPWIND

WIND
SPEED

DIAGRAM 1

APPARENT
WIND
STRENGTH   WIND   BOAT
              STRENGTH SPEED

Right: the dinghy is sailing away from the wind. Its own speed reduces the apparent wind.

colder day with a strong breeze blowing. In a 10-knot wind your boat may be doing something around 5 knots downwind. The speed of the wind over the deck, or the apparent wind, is the difference between the two, i.e. 5 knots. (*diagram 1*).

But if you then change course and sail close hauled, the speed of your boat going into the wind is added to the wind's strength. (When you're sailing close hauled you should be sailing at about 45 degrees to the direction of the natural wind.) If you are sailing at 6 knots, simple geometry shows you that you are making approximately 4 knots directly into the wind (*diagram 2*). Therefore, if the wind is blowing at 10 knots, the wind speed over the deck, the apparent wind, will be 14 knots, or nearly three times as much as before.

Diagram 3 is a vector diagram where the strength of the wind is represented by the lengths of the arrowed lines. It shows that the wind caused by the boat's speed and the natural wind are at an angle to one another. So, unless the boat is sailing directly downwind, the apparent wind is always noticeably closer to the direction in which the boat is sailing than the natural wind.

Note that in the diagram the apparent wind is stronger than the natural wind because the boat's speed is added to it. But, if the apparent wind is coming from aft of the beam, the boat's speed reduces its strength. Therefore you can alter the strength of the apparent wind by altering your course.

A boat which uses the wind efficiently will have the apparent wind further ahead than would a boat that uses it less efficiently. For example, a *470*, or any modern racing dinghy, will sail with its apparent wind further ahead than a cruising dinghy.

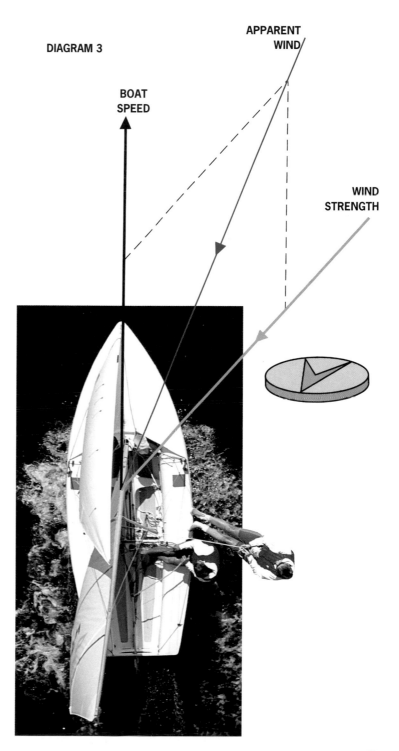

DIAGRAM 3

BOAT SPEED

APPARENT WIND

WIND STRENGTH

Apparent wind 2

The vector diagram on the previous page explained how the angle of the apparent wind is determined by the strength of the natural wind and the speed of the boat through the water. If the speed of the boat increases, but the natural wind remains the same, the apparent wind moves further ahead. Conversely, if the natural wind increases, but the speed of the boat does not, the apparent wind moves further aft.

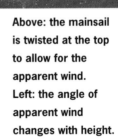

**Above: the mainsail is twisted at the top to allow for the apparent wind.
Left: the angle of apparent wind changes with height.**

APPARENT WIND

Right: waves alter a boat's apparent wind.

However, at water level the natural wind is slowed down by surface friction. At the top of the mast this friction is less significant, so the natural wind blows harder at the top of the mast than at the bottom. As the natural wind increases, so the apparent wind swings aft as shown by the blue/grey arrows in the diagram. This means that the shape of the sail has to alter all the way up the mast so that it corresponds to the changing angle of the apparent wind. This is called twist. The tension on the mainsheet and the angle at which it is set control twist. How it is controlled by the main sheet traveller is explained later.

If the wind always blew with consistent strength and the boat always sailed at constant speed in calm water, the apparent wind would be constant, too. But, not only does the natural wind change in strength and direction, but the boat's speed is also rarely the same. Taking advantage of these factors makes sailing such a skilful and exacting sport. The following examples show how the helmsman should respond when the apparent wind changes.

1 The wind drops in strength, but the boat temporarily keeps its speed. This makes the apparent wind move ahead. The helmsman may think that the natural wind has changed direction. But it has not, and he should maintain his course. As the boat slows down the apparent wind will move aft again.

2 The boat accelerates after a tack. As its speed increases the apparent wind starts to move ahead. To allow for this the helmsman and crew should not haul in the sheets tight immediately. Instead, they must haul them in gradually as the boat accelerates.

3 The boat's speed always increases when it sails down a wave, which makes the apparent wind move ahead, but the boat slows down when climbing a wave and the apparent wind moves aft. To try and keep the apparent wind filling the sails the helmsman alters course, alternately bearing away and luffing up.

Centres of effort and lateral resistance

The sum of all the pressures acting over the entire sail is called the wind force. The wind force can be said to act through a central point in the sail called the centre of effort. The diagrams show the centre of effort for the sail plan, i.e. both sails combined.

The pressure of water on the centreboard produces lateral resistance. Most of this resistance is generated by the centreboard but the rudder and the hull also contribute to it. The sum of these can be regarded as one force acting through one point, just like the wind force in the sail. This point is called the centre of lateral resistance and the *diagrams below* show that it lies somewhere near the aft edge of the centreboard when fully lowered.

To obtain maximum performance, you must keep your dinghy well balanced. Understanding the position of the centre of effort and the centre of lateral resistance in relation to one another will help you do this. To demonstrate how they interact take off the rudder and steer without it. Try this for the first time with an experienced sailor, in light winds, and where there is plenty of room and time to experiment.

Taking off the rudder reduces the lateral resistance at the stern which moves the centre of lateral resistance forwards. If the two forces are not balanced, the boat turns uncontrollably into the wind. To keep the boat sailing on a steady course, the centreboard must be angled back until the two forces are in line again.

The *pictures on the right* show that you can alter course without the rudder just by trimming the sails. To bear away you move the centre of effort ahead by sheeting in the jib and letting out the mainsail. This reduces the drive in the mainsail allowing the wind force in the jib to blow the bow away from the wind. To luff up you reverse the process by sheeting in the mainsail and letting out the jib.

These experiments will show you that it is possible to change direction without the rudder, and to steer the boat just by altering the trim of the sails. If you replace the rudder, you will find that you can use the sails in the same way to help the rudder turn the boat. If you can learn to use the sails in this way, so much the better.

Right: the sequence shows the mainsail full but the wind is being spilled from the jib, so the boat luffs up.

Below right: the sequence shows the jib full but the wind is being spilled from the mainsail, so the boat bears away. In the last picture the boat is close to gybing.

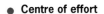

● **Centre of effort**   ● **Centre of lateral resistance**

Both forces are in balance.

Removing the rudder brings the centre of lateral resistance forwards.

Partly raising the centreboard restores the balance of the two forces.

Heeling the boat to steer

Right: this sequence shows, as you can see from the wash, that it is possible to turn quite tightly using crew weight alone. The boat bears away from the wind and then luffs up again sharply.

If you continue to experiment with sailing without a rudder you will soon discover that allowing the boat to heel is another way of steering. This is a powerful effect because two factors are at work here. The centre of effort is to one side, so the wind force will be acting from the side of the boat and tending to push it round. The second factor is that heeling the dinghy over alters its underwater profile. (This is the shape that would be seen by a fish from below.) Normally it has two curved sides, just as the boat is curved. But if one side is sunk deeply into the water it becomes asymmetrical. This creates a turning shape. If you dig in the leeward side, the boat will turn rapidly into the wind. And vice versa.

If you use this effect combined with subtle sail adjustment, you will be able to manoeuvre the dinghy minus the rudder surprisingly effectively. It is quite amusing to try this and it is an excellent way of learning the feel of your boat. The pictures (*left*) show a sequence of a dinghy being steered in this way.

The purpose of the sailing without a rudder exercise has been to show that the boat will tend to turn if the wind force and water force are not in balance. In practice they often diverge and the rudder has to be used to compensate. The rudder works by slowing down one side of the boat relative to the other, so every time it is used some speed will be lost. So the moral is to keep the forces as balanced as possible. When out of balance, a boat which tends to turn away from the wind is said to have lee helm because you have to compensate by pushing the tiller to leeward. The reverse situation is known as weather helm.

When sailing normally you need the rudder for fine control, but you can use these effects to help the rudder to turn the boat and this is what experienced sailors try to do. For example, when trying to bear away it helps considerably if you ease the main sheet first. When making a racing tack the crew lets the boat heel to encourage it to come up into the wind and once it has passed the eye of the wind to heel it the other way to help it to bear away. Likewise, heeling the boat to windward before a gybe will speed up the turn.

An example of weather helm is shown in the picture where the boat has deliberately been allowed to heel too much and it is trying to turn up into the wind. The helmsman has to apply strong corrective action! It is wasteful to use the rudder to correct a dinghy heeling when a good crew would keep it upright.

You should set up your boat so that it sails normally with the tiller pointing directly up the boat indicating good balance. The rake of the mast should be set up correctly on shore, although in some classes it can be adjusted on the water. We have shown how the trim of the sails can effect the position of the centre of effort, but their shape can do this also. For example, the mainsail will distort in strong winds and the centre of effort will move aft as the sail bellies out in the middle. The Cunningham control (described later) is used to pull the centre of effort forwards again.

Left: the boat has been deliberately allowed to heel too far, so correction with the rudder has to be applied.

Above: this J24 has heeled over so much that the rudder is totally ineffective.

SAILS AND RIGGING
Cutting sails

Left: a curve has been marked on the bottom edge of a length of sailcloth according to the sailmaker's pattern.

Double-sided sticky tape is then applied to the line and the sailmaker cuts the cloth to make the shape of a panel.

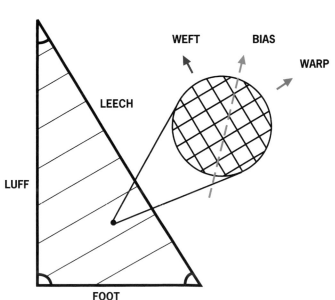

Left: diagram shows a magnified section of sail cloth and how it is aligned to resist stretch at the leech.

Above: the panel's curving edge is shown adjacent to the straight edge of the next panel which is about to be attached to it.

The sails and rigging of a dinghy are its motor. To change gear, as it were, a helmsman needs to be able to alter the shape of a mainsail in order to control the amount of wind in it. For instance, if the wind is very strong he can decrease the wind force by reducing the sail's curvature. He does this by stretching it with the sail controls described later. The sail's curvature and its stretch characteristics are therefore very important.

A sail is made up of panels of woven polyester cloth which are cut to be wider in the middle than at the ends. So when they are sewn together curvature is introduced into the sail. For demonstration purposes, this effect has been exaggerated in these pictures where two panels are being taped together prior to stitching by the sailmaker.

The polyester cloth is impregnated, or coated, to prevent it from stretching excessively. It is made of threads that are woven horizontally and vertically, known respectively as the weft and the warp. All woven cloth tends to be more stable in the weft and warp, but less stable – that is more stretchable – in the diagonal direction known as the bias (*see diagram*).

The greatest stress in a mainsail occurs at its leech where it is not supported by the boom or mast. The panels are therefore sewn together to ensure that either the weft or warp runs parallel with the leech. This means that the edges of the panels that meet the mast and the boom are closer to the angle of the bias of the material and the sail can be stretched more readily along its luff and foot by the sail controls.

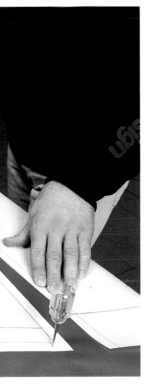

Right: the two panels are stuck together with sticky tape prior to stitching. The curvature in the sail can be clearly seen.

A sail's shape

Above left: the mainsail laid out flat on the sail loft floor with the luff curve visible.

Above right: the mainsail has been allowed to curve in the middle. The luff is straight.

Opposite page right: the same sail on the sailmaker's test rig. The luff is straight.

Opposite page left: the rig curves the luff and flattens the sail.

Because of the curvature created by the shaped panels, a sail never lies completely flat. The pictures directly above show this. On the left a mainsail has been laid out on the sail loft floor and it can be seen that its luff has taken up a curve. But if the sail is billowed, as it has been on the right, to make the middle part rise off the floor, the luff is nearly straight and only a small amount of curvature remains. This is because of the way the front edges of the panels are shaped by the sailmaker. It is his skill and experience which determines the balance between them.

When a sail is hoisted on a straight mast, curvature is introduced into it. But masts are made to flex and the pictures at the top of the opposite page show how this can be reproduced by a sailmaker's test rig. The spar representing the mast can be pulled into

different shapes by the tackle on the supporting bars. If the spar is straight the sail takes up its curvature. If the spar is bent the sail is flattened and the luff takes up a similar curve to the one where it is lying on the sail loft floor in the first picture in the sequence.

The left hand picture on the page opposite shows that the luff has a slight curve. This is because the sailmaker has shaped the front of the panels so that the sail matches the intended shape of the mast.

When cutting the jib the sailmaker allows for an inward curve on the luff because it sags when set, as will be seen later.

It is the combination of the luff curve and the shaping of the panel seams which gives the curvature in the sail. A sailmaker must know the bending characteristics of the mast so that the sail can be matched to it.

Sails are produced with a standard amount of curvature built in by the sailmaker. This curvature is defined in terms of the cross section of the sail. The point of maximum depth in its curvature is known as the draft position. Both the amount of depth and its position can be varied for different wind and sea conditions as the diagrams show.

Normally, when sailing to windward, a shape with a fine entry – a flattened curve at the luff – will give good pointing ability, so the draft position is nearly halfway back (1).

When sailing off the wind, pointing ability is irrelevant, so the draft position is moved forwards which gives the sail more depth and increased power (2).

In very strong winds the sail is flattened to reduce the power and to keep the boat under careful control (3).

——— **CHORD**
------ **DRAFT POSITION**

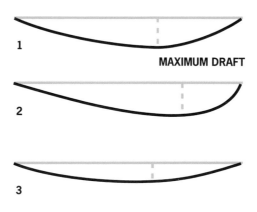

MAXIMUM DRAFT

1

2

3

Left: (top) the chord and depth at the point of maximum curvature have been superimposed on a mainsail. The diagrams (below) show ideal shapes for different conditions.

Mast bend and spreaders

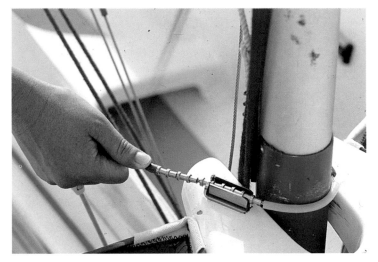

To alter the shape of the mainsail, and to control the wind in it, a mast can be made to bend in both a fore and aft direction, as well as sideways. These bending characteristics are determined by the mast maker.

A modern metal mast is wider in the fore and aft direction to give it stiffness and is narrower laterally to try and minimise the turbulence it always creates at the luff of the mainsail. It is tapered towards its top to give the top section necessary increased flexibility and also to save weight.

To make a mast bend properly it is important to ensure that it cannot move at the

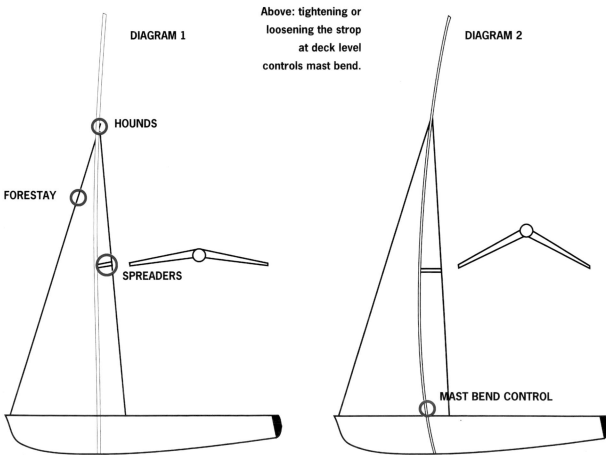

DIAGRAM 1

Above: tightening or loosening the strop at deck level controls mast bend.

DIAGRAM 2

HOUNDS

FORESTAY

SPREADERS

MAST BEND CONTROL

heel where it is firmly fixed to the boat. The mast is also fixed at the hounds where the forestay and the shrouds meet it. Consequently, when the top section of the mast is bent aft the middle section bends forwards.

The degree to which the mast can bend is controlled at deck level. Different boats have different methods. The *470* has a wire strop which presses on the front of the mast. If the strop is tight, the mast cannot move forwards at deck level and this restricts bend. Loosening the strop allows the mast to bend more. The more the bend the flatter the sail, which in turn controls the wind force in it.

Because the shrouds help support the mast, the angle created in them by the spreaders has a significant effect on mast bend. The shrouds are always set up taut and this tension is always trying to straighten the angle caused by the spreaders. The spreaders are normally set to deflect the shrouds slightly aft so that their tension will bend the mast a little anyway (*diagram 1*). Angling the spreaders further aft increases the bend in the mast and flattens the sail more (*diagram 2*).

The ability of the mast to bend sideways controls the response of the sails to a gust. Imagine the boat sailing with the maximum amount of power that the crew can handle. If a gust suddenly hits, it bends the top section of the mast sideways. This makes the sail twist away from the wind at the top allowing the wind to escape. This is known as 'twisting off'. When the gust subsides the mast straightens up and the sail once more can extract maximum power from the wind.

When the top section of the mast bends sideways the leeward shroud goes slack and the middle section bows to windward (*diagram 3*). This movement is resisted by the windward

DIAGRAM 3   **DIAGRAM 4**

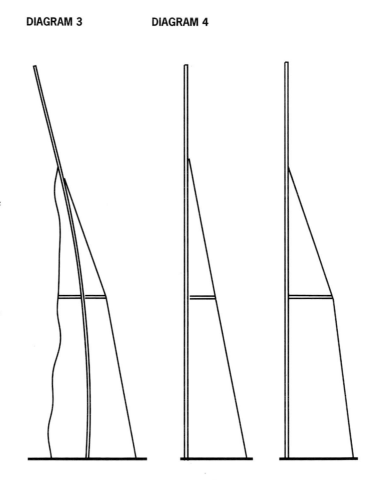

spreader. Lengthening the spreaders creates additional tension in the shrouds and this stiffens the mast considerably (*diagram 4*). Lightweight crews would normally have shorter spreaders than heavy crews as this allows the top of the mast to bend more and so the sail twists off more readily, releasing excess wind force which only the weight of a heavy crew could counterbalance.

Because a gust causes the middle of the mast to bend to windward, it also keeps the slot clear when it would otherwise by obstructed by the mainsail bellying out in its middle.

71

The Cunningham

Dinghy rigs have black bands on the mast and boom to mark the points which have been measured to the class rules. To ensure fair competition it is not permitted to pull the sail beyond these bands. One of the bands limits the height to which a mainsail can be hoisted. When hoisted to it the mainsail's luff is still fairly slack. To tension it a device called the Cunningham is used.

Named after its inventor, the Cunningham consists of a line run through a hole, or cringle, in the mainsail which is positioned just above the boom. When the wind increases the mainsail tends to belly in the middle, which moves the point of maximum draft in the sail

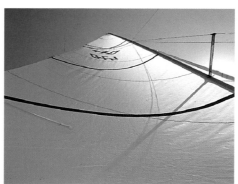

Above left: the line that pulls down on the luff is fully released.
Far left and left: the Cunningham is not creating any tension. It is just being used to gather up the creases in the luff. The views from astern, looking up the sail and down from the masthead show that the point of maximum curvature is towards the middle of the sail.

aft making it inefficient and difficult to handle. Increasing the tension on the luff by hauling in on the Cunningham line pulls the sail forwards and therefore brings the point of maximum draft forwards to its correct position. This tensioning by the Cunningham also makes the sail twist off at the top, so the line is also used to reduce the wind force in the sail and therefore reduce the tendency to heel.

These pictures are taken on a close hauled course. On a run or a reach the Cunningham is released. The only exception would be when reaching in very strong winds. It can then be pulled in hard to twist off the top of the sail and dispose of excess wind force.

Above: the line is pulled tight and the luff is tensioned. Right and far right: the Cunningham is fully on. The views from astern, looking up the sail and down from the masthead show that the point of maximum curvature has been brought forward, and the top of the sail has twisted off.

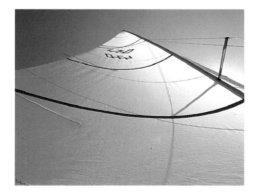

The outhaul

Right: the outhaul is being adjusted. Below: the outhaul is on and the camber stripes on the sail show that the curvature has been reduced for sailing to windward.

The outhaul controls the tension along the foot of the sail. It is a line attached to a cringle at the clew of the sail which is normally led forward through the inside of the boom to a point near the gooseneck where it can be easily adjusted when sailing.

The outhaul can be marked using a waterproof felt tip pen. There is a scale on the boom and, when you have found the right setting for a particular wind strength, the position of the mark against the scale can be noted. The tension on the outhaul can then be readily repeated when the same wind conditions recur. It is good practice to do this when using any of the control lines.

Pulling in the outhaul increases the tension in the foot of the sail and reduces its curvature lower down. Page 34, on the sail's shape, showed the different curvatures required for different points of sailing. The outhaul is normally pulled in for windward work to give the sail a shape with a fine entry. This improves a dinghy's pointing ability, but when sailing downwind the outhaul is released to give the sail more depth and more power.

The outhaul is also adjusted for different wind strengths. If the wind is too strong it is kept tight to flatten the lower part of the sail and reduce the wind force. The same applies in very light winds. This is because if there is insufficient airflow to follow a large curve, turbulence will set in. Flattening the sail helps what little airflow exists to be coaxed gently round it for maximum effect.

Below: the outhaul is released and the camber stripes show that the curvature has been increased for sailing downwind.

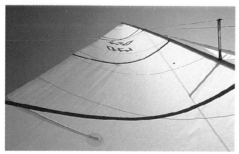

Kicking strap or boom vang

The kicking strap is often called the kicker for short, and is also known as the vang. It runs from a point about a third of the way along the boom to the foot of the mast. A series of pulley blocks increase the purchase so that a powerful pull can be exerted. Normally the line is led back to the centre of the boat and then out to each side deck. It must be near to hand because it has to be operated very simply and quickly in strong winds.

Its effect is to pull down on the sail and tighten the leech, which will reduce the twist in the sail. At the same time, it forces the boom

Above: the kicking strap. Right and far right: the kicking strap has been pulled in tight. Notice how the boom is pulled down and how this tensions the leech.

forwards and encourages the mast to bend. So, if the wire strop holding the mast has been released, the centre of the mast will move forwards and this flattens the sail.

When sailing close hauled, pulling the main sheet in tight will have a similar effect, because most of its pull is downwards and normally the kicking strap will hang loosely. But in strong winds the main sheet has to be eased. Then the kicking strap is used to keep the sail in shape and to maintain control when the wind is spilled from it. Normally, when sailing off wind, it would be pulled in tight, which will keep the

end of the boom low and expose the maximum sail area to the wind. In the event of a strong gust, releasing the kicking strap allows the boom to rise, the leech to slacken, and the top of the sail to twist off and so release the sudden excess power.

If your boat has its main sheet attached to the aft end of the boom rather than the central arrangement featured in the dinghy here, it is essential to use the kicking strap when sailing downwind. If you do not, the boom rises and the mainsail bellies out so much that it becomes completely uncontrollable.

Left and far left: the kicking strap has been released. Notice how the leech has slackened and the sail is twisting towards the top.

The main sheet traveller and sail twist

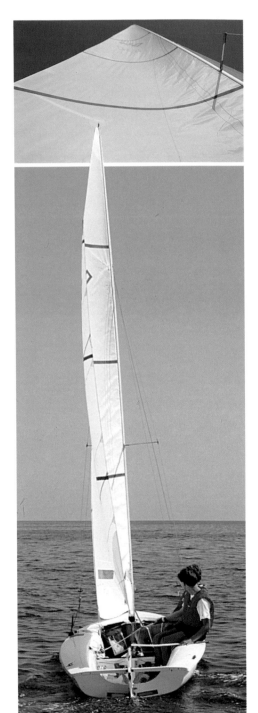

Amongst dinghy classes there is a wide variety of different main sheet systems. This *470* has its main sheet block mounted on a metal hoop which can be pulled across the boat. Its purpose is to alter the angle that the main sheet pulls downwards on the boom. The front of the boom is supported by the gooseneck on the mast, so any downwards pressure will tend to pull the aft end of the boom down which in turn puts tension in the leech. Just as a washing line becomes straighter when pulled out harder so does the leech of a sail. As the apparent wind changes direction with the height of the sail, the angle of the sail has to change, too, and it twists.

Setting the hoop well up to windward reduces tension in the leech, as the main sheet is pulling mostly sideways. Setting it to leeward while sheeting in increases the tension, because the main sheet is pulling mostly downwards. Sailing to windward, the boom should be on the centre line, and the leech should curve gradually all the way up.

In gusts, tension in the leech is reduced to allow the top of the sail to twist off.

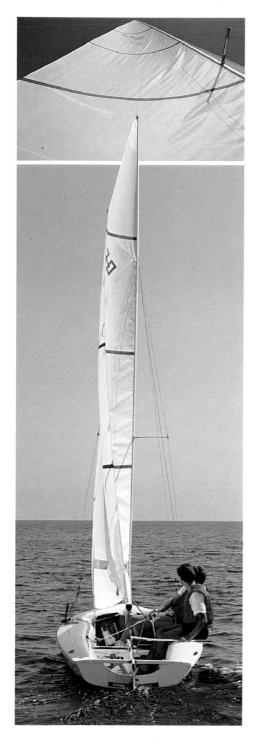

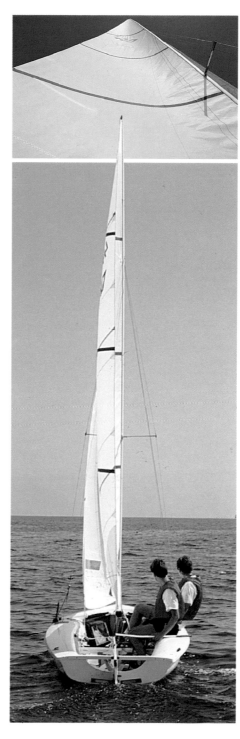

Left: the mainsheet hoop has been set centrally in the boat and the main sheet pulled in tight. Notice how the leech is straightened.

Far left: the hoop has been pulled up to windward and the main sheet let out so that the boom is once more on the centre line. Notice how the sail twists excessively.

Controlling the jib

Right and below: the fairlead is too far forwards and the top telltale is lifting, indicating that the leech is too tight.

Above: front view of the dinghy showing the sag in the forestay when the jib halyard is released. The sails are cut to allow for a certain amount of sag, but the halyard should be tighter than this.

The jib always sags to leeward because it is rigged on the forestay which flexes according to the tension the mast puts on it. The sailmaker cuts the sail to allow for this by giving its luff an inward curve not an outward curve as he does with the mainsail.

The picture on the *far left* shows the jib sagging too much because the jib halyard is too loose. Tightening the halyard straightens the sail's inward curve and therefore reduces the sag. It also flattens the sail and so has the same result on the jib as bending the centre section of the mast has on the mainsail.

When sailing off the wind the jib sheets are used to trim the sail, but when sailing to windward the crew leaves the sheet cleated in position. The tension on the sheet determines the curvature in the sail. In medium winds and flat water the tension is increased by sheeting in to flatten the sail. This gives the boat the ability to head closer to the wind which is known as pointing ability. When sailing in rough seas, where power is required more than pointing ability, the jib is sheeted more loosely.

The position of the jib fairlead also affects the shape of the jib. The further forwards it is positioned, the more it pulls the sheet down, thus tightening the leech and giving good pointing ability. If it is too far forwards, however, the jib will obstruct the slot and backwind the mainsail.

The further aft the fairlead is positioned the more the sheet pulls laterally, which increases the tension along the foot of the sail. This releases the tension in the leech, allowing it to twist more. In strong winds the fairlead is pulled aft to allow the jib to twist off if necessary. In very light winds more twist is required, so the fairlead is set aft to allow the jib to follow the shape of the mainsail.

Setting the sail controls correctly

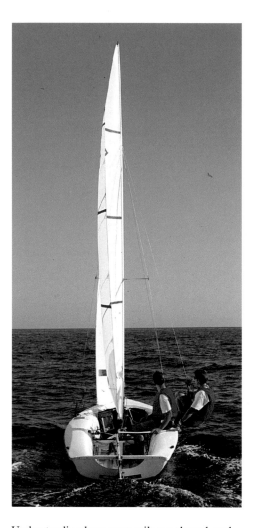

Understanding how your sails are shaped, and how this shape can be altered in various ways, is essential if you are to get the best out of your dinghy, or, indeed, any sailing boat.

Some examples of how the controls should be set under different wind conditions are explained here, but there are no hard and fast rules on sail control. The only way to discover what is exactly right is to go out on to the water and experiment.

These pictures show the *470* with its controls set up correctly for sailing to windward in medium winds and reasonably calm water. These are ideal conditions for making good progress, and the sails are fairly flat so that the boat can point close to the wind. The jib fairlead is set midway and the jib sheet is pulled in fairly tight. The main boom is on the centre line of the boat and the mainsail has a little twist. The outhaul is tight but the Cunningham is only pulled in slightly.

If the sea becomes rough, both the mainsail and jib sheets as well as the outhaul are eased a little to obtain, at the expense of pointing ability, more power to drive through and over the waves. Though not sailing as close to the wind, you are able to maintain your speed and minimise leeway.

In exceptionally light conditions, it is difficult to maintain sufficient airflow, so the curvature in the sails has to be reduced a little. The mast is allowed to bend forwards in the middle by releasing the wire strop. The outhaul is pulled in tight to flatten the foot of the sail and the Cunningham is left slack. Although unsightly creases will appear in the luff of the sail, do not be concerned about them - they will not make any difference to your performance. Additional twist is required in these conditions, so the traveller is pulled to windward and the jib fairlead pulled aft.

In strong winds, the objective is to reduce the heeling force by flattening the sail as the crew weight will be insufficient to keep the boat upright. The wire strop is released and the kicking strap is pulled on very hard to bend the mast. The outhaul is pulled in tight and the Cunningham is employed to twist off the top of the sail. But if there is still too much wind force in the sail, you must release the mainsheet. In really big gusts the crew may have to release the jib as well.

83

Care of sails

Above and above right: out on the water rolling up mainsail.

You should treat your sails with care; they will then last longer and perform better.

Sails should not be allowed to flap too much because this will break down the impregnated resin, and the creases will impair the performance of the sail. Salt is harmful to sails and ideally they should be washed down after being used at sea, but make sure you have somewhere suitable to dry them. Allowing them to flap like washing on a line is definitely not good! Do not smoke when handling sails. The wind can easily blow off a piece of hot ash which will burn a neat little hole.

Where possible you should roll up your sails after use. The two pictures above show the mainsail being rolled up and then tied while the boat is still on the water. The halyard is detached and the sail rolled up from its head downwards. Finally, the main sheet is tied round the sail to keep it rolled while the crew take a break.

The three pictures *below* show how you roll up the mainsail with one person at each end. The same procedure applies for a cruising boat or a dinghy except that you can only leave the sail on the boom if you possess a sail cover to

Below: sequence shows a cruiser mainsail being rolled up and tied.

protect it from the sun's ultra violet light. Here the mainsail is secured with sail ties before the cover is pulled over.

When coming ashore try to drop the mainsail so that it falls over the boom, first to one side and then the other, as the picture on the left in the sequence *above* shows. This is known as flaking. The sail can then be rolled up, easily removed from the boom, and stored in the bag. If the jib has a luff wire, you have to wind the wire round in a smooth circle. Then it is ready to go in the bag.

As a sail ages the resin breaks down and the effect of this is a dramatic increase in the stretch of the sail along the bias of the cloth. This means that the sail will belly out, particularly in strong winds, which is just when you need a flatter shape. Keeping old sails for use in strong winds is therefore not a way to make your sailing easier. You should regularly examine the sails for wear or chafe. Any small tears should be mended immediately before they become large ones. If a sailmaker is not available to repair them, use strong adhesive tape or sew them up yourself as a temporary measure.

Above: sequence shows mainsail being flaked and then rolled and bagged.
Below far left: coiling the jib luff wire.
Below left: some jibs have a roller which allows you to wrap the foresail around itself just by pulling a line. Here the same effect is being achieved by detaching the jib sheets and wrapping them round.

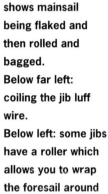

ADVANCED TECHNIQUES
Setting the spinnaker

Now that you know how to set up your sails perfectly for the prevailing conditions, it is time to introduce you to the more advanced aspects of sailing. Knowing how to handle and set your spinnaker correctly is important because it is a sail that will make your time out on the water that much more interesting. Trapeze technique is also important and will add considerably to the performance of a dinghy. Then, high speed planing and the three sail reach will show you just how exciting sailing can be!

Above: sequence shows how the spinnaker hook is correctly inserted into the eye on the mast. When the string is released, the plunger locks the pole into place. The uphaul/ downhaul is attached to the pole by the hook.

The spinnaker is kept in a bag. There are two of these, positioned on either side of the boat in the front of the cockpit. It is easier to hoist the spinnaker if it is packed in the leeward bag, so it helps to try and predict what the wind direction will be at the time when you want to use a spinnaker.

Some dinghies overcome this problem by hoisting the spinnaker from a chute in the bow. In fact, there are several methods to make spinnaker handling easier, some of which are very complicated! The class rules of the *470* only allow a relatively simple system. But at least it is less likely to go wrong!

It can be rather embarrassing and time-consuming to hoist the spinnaker with a twist in it, so check it on land beforehand. The sail has a red stripe on one side and a green one down the other. Choose one side and pass it from top to bottom through your hands. If one side is untwisted, the other will be also and the sail

will hoist smoothly and cleanly.

The spinnaker is a very light sail and it needs a pole for it to set properly. The pole has a hook at each end with a plunger which holds it in position. The plungers are operated by a string.

The height of the pole is adjusted by a continuous line, of which the upper part is known as the uphaul, because it holds the pole up. The lower part, the downhaul, prevents the wind force in the spinnaker lifting the pole too high. The ends are fixed to the pole by means of a hook, which can easily be slipped on and off.

The spinnaker is hoisted by its own halyard. This is led back along the floor of the boat, so the helmsman can operate it. A rope is attached to each of the spinnaker's clews. To distinguish between them, the rope attached on the same side as the pole is called the guy; the other is known as the sheet. When gybing the pole is changed to the other side and the names of the sheet and guy are reversed. They are still the same ropes but the name change indicates the change in function.

When setting the spinnaker you must expose as much of the sail as possible to the windward side. This increases the forward drive of the sail. The crew has to give complete attention to trimming the sheet correctly so that the luff is constantly on the point of collapsing. If it starts to fall in, a quick tweak will bring it back out again, but you have to act quickly.

For a run and a reach there are different settings. On a run the spinnaker should be set so that both the clews are at an equal height. On a reach the pole is brought forward and usually raised a little. It is most important that the air flows cleanly from the leech of the spinnaker or turbulence will set in.

Below left: spinnaker correctly set for a reach with (inset) view from masthead. Below: spinnaker correctly set for a run with (inset) view from masthead.

Hoisting and dropping the spinnaker on a reach

1

2

3

**HOISTING ON
A REACH**

It is easier to hoist the spinnaker from the leeward side, and that is the method shown here. It is possible to hoist it from the windward side, but you will have to manoeuvre the spinnaker round the front of the forestay as you do so, otherwise it will fill behind the jib instead of in front of it.

The sequence is as follows: the crew picks up the spinnaker pole. Holding it the right way up, she clips the spinnaker guy into the end (1). She then clips the pole's uphaul/downhaul rope onto the centre of the pole (2) She can then push the pole forwards (3). The downhaul rope is tensioned by means

1

2

3

**LOWERING ON
A REACH**

When lowering the spinnaker on a reach it is much easier to pull the sail down on the windward side, and this is the rule that is usually followed. The helmsman takes over the job of trimming the spinnaker sheet, while the

crew removes the pole from the mast (1). With the pole off the mast, she can then bring it back into the boat (2), and, now able to reach the uphaul/ downhaul, she can unclip it from the pole (3).

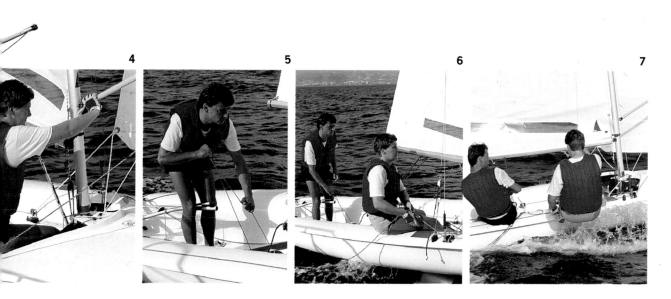

4   5   6   7

of an elastic 'shockcord' so that it can be extended just far enough for the inboard end of the pole to be clipped to the mast (4).

The spinnaker is now ready to hoist. This is the job of the helmsman who first stands up controlling the rudder with his legs. He then has two free hands and is able to pull the halyard up very rapidly and get back to steering the boat properly (5). At the same time as the spinnaker leaves the bag, the crew is pulling the guy round and cleating it in position (6). The crew then takes over the spinnaker sheet and starts to trim it. As the boat picks up speed, she starts to move her weight outboard (7).

4

5

6

She stows the pole in the bottom of the boat and reaches forwards to grab the spinnaker guy and pulls it in (4). She pulls the spinnaker round with the cooperation of the helmsman. He has to let out the sheet at the right time (5).

The crew gathers the sail and the helmsman releases the halyard so that she can pull it down and stow it in the bag (6).

Hoisting and dropping the spinnaker on a run

When the spinnaker is hoisted on a reach, the pole has to be positioned first. This is because the pole is required to hold the sail as soon as it has been pulled out of the bag, otherwise the spinnaker would blow off to leeward out of control. But, when hoisted on a run, however, the spinnaker will fill ahead of the boat, and does so without much force because it is shielded by the mainsail. This means that the helmsman does not have to wait for the crew to set the pole before hoisting the spinnaker, and he can also hoist it on the windward side as this sequence shows.

1 The helmsman stands up and steers with the tiller between his legs thus releasing both hands so he can first work the halyard and then the sheets. The crew reaches for the pole and clips on the guy.

2 The helmsman hoists the sail while the crew reaches for the uphaul hook so that she can clip on the uphaul and downhaul.

3 The helmsman takes the sheet in his hand and adjusts it while the crew pushes out the pole and attaches the inboard end of the pole to the mast.

4 The helmsman ensures that the sail is pulling before he hands the sheet to the crew and then he sits on the leeward side deck. He does this to give the crew a better view of the sail and to make it easier for her to trim it correctly.

When lowering the spinnaker the procedure is reversed.

5 The helmsman stands again ready to steer with his legs.

6 He takes over control of the sheet while the crew takes the pole off the spinnaker and the mast, detaches the uphaul and downhaul, and brings the pole inboard.

7 The helmsman holds the halyard ready to release it while the crew gathers the foot of the sail together and checks the halyard is free.

8 The helmsman releases the halyard and eases both the halyard and the sheet so that the crew is able to pull the sail down without it dropping into the water. The sail is then returned to the spinnaker bag.

5

6

7

8

Gybing the spinnaker

Gybing has already been explained, but this time you have the added complication of changing sides with the spinnaker pole as well. The guy and the sheet will now exchange their names, because their functions will change.

There are many different methods of dealing a spinnaker pole when you are gybing with the spinnaker up. Some people take off the pole before gybing the boat. Others clip the mast end of the pole onto the sail, so that it is attached to both corners of the spinnaker. If the pole is relatively light, it is possible to gybe first and then change the pole over afterwards which is the method shown in this sequence. The

The helmsman stands and takes hold of both guy and sheet. The crew releases the guy from its jamming cleat.

The helmsman is now controlling the spinnaker. The crew pulls on the kicking strap.

They both duck as the main boom comes across.

The main boom continues to swing out and you can see the pole still attached to the spinnaker.

measure of a good gybe is that the sail is kept filled and flying throughout.

Although you can sail in any direction without a spinnaker, you would be missing one of the most challenging aspects of sailing if you did not use it. For it not only increases your speed but it also makes your sailing much more interesting. It has a large sail area and often seems to have a mind of its own. These pictures make it look easy, but hoisting the spinnaker often causes problems and, because it is set flying in front of the boat, rather than attached to spars, it can collapse at a moment's notice and needs constant attention.

The crew releases the pole from the spinnaker by unclipping it. She detaches the pole from the mast, but leaves the uphaul still attached.

The crew attaches the spinnaker pole to the sail and pushes it out on the new side.

Having attached the pole to the mast fitting the crew takes over the guy (the old sheet) and cleats it in position.

The crew takes hold of the sheet (the old guy) to trim the sail as the helmsman sits to leeward.

The trapeze

The trapeze helps combat a dinghy's heeling force by giving the crew greater leverage to counterbalance the wind force in the sails. The more the crew's weight is moved outboard to windward the greater the wind force which can be maintained in the sails. The greater the wind force the greater the speed.

The trapeze is simply a wire connected at the hounds at one end and to a harness the crew wears at the other. The best types give good back support. Use gripping tape on the boat's gunwales where the crew's feet will be. Non-

Left and below left: good technique – keep your feet together and your body straight. You can use your arm to support your neck because it can get tired after a while. Below and bottom: wrong techniques – do not bend forwards and hang onto the handle.

slip shoes should be worn by the crew.

The crew's front leg is always braced to avoid being swung forwards, but the back leg can be relaxed slightly. The crew's height above the water can be altered by adjusting the length of the trapeze. The maximum leverage is obtained by staying as horizontal as possible. Moving in and out every time the wind drops or lifts a little can be tiring, so in fluctuating winds the wire is raised to decrease the crew's leverage. It is also raised in rough seas to stop the crew hitting the water.

Below: the trapeze has a system of pulleys and a jamming cleat which enables you to adjust its length and therefore your height.
Right: you gain the most leverage if you stay as horizontal as possible.
Below right: in rough seas you should be raised higher otherwise you will hit the waves!

The trapeze: moving in and out

Using the trapeze is a little daunting at first, but it makes sailing much more exciting. It is easier if you follow the proper technique for moving in and out when tacking as demonstrated here.

The crew is suspended on the wire with the jib sheet in her hands (1). She grasps the trapeze handle, bends her knees, and starts to come inboard (2). The wire is still supporting her as she aims her front leg into the boat (3). Having unhooked the wire she starts to step over the centreboard case (4). She crosses under the boom and changes the jib sheets. You can see the new trapeze wire held in position by a shockcord (5). Sitting on the deck, she grasps the wire and pulls it towards her (6). She hooks on (7). She pushes out with her front leg keeping the back leg straight to maintain balance. This is important (8). Still holding the handle she pushes out ready to settle into position for the new tack (9).

Pushing out as as seen from above:
Hooking on to the trapeze wire (1B). Pushing out from the deck with front leg, with back leg straight (2B). Halfway out, still holding the handle until balance is achieved (3B).
Coming back in as seen from above:
Fully out, with handle released, front leg braced, and back leg relaxed (4B). Halfway back in with back leg straight (5B). Back on board, unclipping the hook (6B).

Right: it takes agility to move in and out on the trapeze but it makes for an exhilarating sail.

Planing

When sailing normally, a boat creates its own wave which it carries along with it. The faster it goes the longer and deeper this wave becomes. But this wave cannot exceed the length of the boat so, when its second crest has reached the stern, the boat has reached its theoretical maximum speed. It can only go faster by breaking out of its wave and riding on top of it. This is known as planing.

This picture shows a *470* on a plane. Its speed has increased to the point where it has risen onto its bow wave and has lifted the forward part of the hull out of the water.

Dinghies capable of planing are designed with flattened sections aft and the water pressure there supports the boat. This has two beneficial effects: the surface area is reduced, which lessens the water's frictional resistance on the hull; and the wake has flattened leaving little wash, which means less energy is wasted on making waves.

As a boat starts to plane the crew move aft to maintain the boat's balance. It takes more energy to get the boat up onto the plane than to hold it there, so the crew should pump the sails in and out while moving aft. As the boat accelerates the sheets are pulled in. The increase in speed is dramatic, and the apparent wind will move ahead.

The boat has to be kept upright, because it never planes unless it is presenting its hull sections at the correct angle to the water. But, once it is in the groove, as it were, the water pressure should help the boat to feel quite stable. The centreboard is partially raised. If a gust hits, the helmsman bears away to bring the wind astern and reduce the heeling effect. If the wind drops, it helps maintain the momentum if he luffs up to bring the apparent wind ahead.

The weight moves aft on a plane to maintain stability and balance.

Sailing in waves

Above: crew weight should be well back when planing downwind.

Right: from above it can be seen how the crew has angled herself back on the trapeze line, so that she is in line with the helmsman.

Below: sequence shows how the helmsman and crew move their weight forwards when climbing a wave and back as they surf down one.

Opposite: the bow of the boat rises as it climbs the wave.

Planing downwind in waves is even more exciting than in calm water. The idea is to surf down the front of a wave and pick up enough speed to climb up the back of the next one.

When a wave begins lifting the boat, the helmsman and crew move their weight forward to encourage the boat to tip over its crest. As the boat accelerates down the face of the wave, they move back. This raises the bow and encourages the boat to keep planing all the way up and over the next wave. The helmsman bears away as the boat rides down the wave. He then luffs up to increase the apparent wind. This increases the wind force in the sails which helps the boat climb up the next one.

When sailing to windward close hauled in waves, the helmsman and crew keep close to each other to reduce wind resistance. This is critical, otherwise the boat will crash into the waves, not move smoothly over them. In the sequence of pictures *below* you can see that the heads of the helmsman and crew of a well sailed boat move up and down far less than the bow and stern. Their weight and position act as a pivot and this ensures that energy is not

wasted. In the picture *opposite* taken from above the boat, you can see how the crew has angled herself back to achieve this.

When sailing to windward in waves, the helmsman uncleats the mainsheet so that he can be constantly trimming it to control the power. He keeps it in tight to extract as much driving force as possible. But if the boat starts to heel, the helmsman must spill excess wind force by releasing the sheet.

Three sail reaching

This picture shows an exciting three sail reach. As long as you keep the boat level you can just about stay in control and enjoy the ride. But, if the boat heels, the spinnaker's centre of effort moves over the leeward side which pulls the boat up into the wind. This is known as a broach and in a dinghy it is usually followed by a capsize. To avoid this the helmsman and crew must keep their weight right out, easing the sheets to spill wind if necessary, and in a strong gust the helmsman may have to release the main sheet to depower the mainsail, and release the kicking strap too. If that is insufficient, the crew must release the spinnaker sheet.

Provided there is room to do so, the helmsman can lessen the effect of a gust by turning the boat further away from the wind which reduces the heeling effect and the strength of the apparent wind. To do this the bow needs to be well clear of the waves to stop it digging in on the leeward side which would prevent the boat from turning. To ensure that it is clear, the crew weight has to be well back. In the picture the spinnaker is trimmed with the pole well forwards. As the wind has lifted the sail, the pole is raised to keep both clews of the spinnaker level.

A three sail reach is much faster than running directly before the wind. So it is often quicker to sail to a point directly downwind of you by taking a longer, zigzag, course which you do by alternately reaching and gybing until you reach your destination. However, doing this does depend on the wind strength, and the type of boat you are sailing. In strong winds it seems to pay off for any boat that will plane. Catamaran sailors always do it, even in light winds. It is more comfortable too; running directly downwind in large seas makes a boat roll and difficult to steer accurately.

CRUISER SAILING
Introducing the *J24*

1 **Pulpit**
2 **Pushpit**
3 **Lifelines**
4 **Foredeck**
5 **Fore hatch**
6 **Cabin hatch**
7 **Cockpit**
8 **Chainplate**
9 **Mooring cleat**
10 **Bow fairlead**
11 **Outboard bracket**
12 **Kicking strap**
13 **Main sheet traveller**
14 **Halyard winch**
15 **Sheet winches**
Continued opposite

This section deals with sailing in a keel boat. Many of the same rules apply, so the section concentrates on those aspects that are different to sailing a dinghy. However, some subjects, like tacking and gybing, are repeated because boat handling is important.

The *J24* is a lightweight cruiser/racer, but even so it weighs more than 10 times as much as the *470*. This means the sails have to generate more power, so they are larger in area and the mast is more substantial. The sails sometimes generate such power that winches are needed to haul in the sheets and they are also used for the halyards.

Since the mast is heavier, there has to be more rigging to support it. So there is a backstay as well as a forestay and there are extra shrouds which terminate half way up the

mast. These are fixed to substantial chainplates which extend well inside the hull to withstand the large strains imposed. When the mainsail is not hoisted the boom has to be supported by a wire called the topping lift.

There is a bracket for mounting an outboard engine, which would normally be carried for cruising but taken off for racing. Invaluable for getting you home if the wind drops, the engine should also be used when coming into marinas. Handling a boat under sail in such confined spaces is sometimes very difficult because the wind is variable. Emergencies can happen quickly. Remember that at low speeds the keel loses its effect and you would risk drifting helplessly sideways and hitting something if you don't use the engine.

The *J24* has a small cabin below with

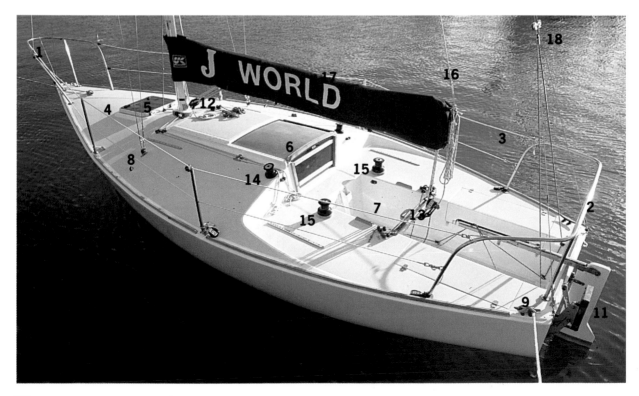

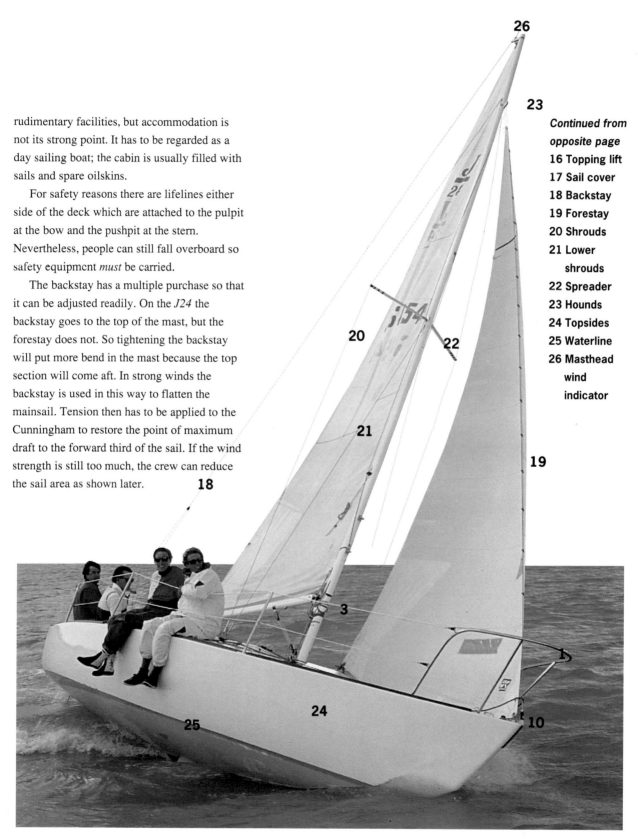

rudimentary facilities, but accommodation is not its strong point. It has to be regarded as a day sailing boat; the cabin is usually filled with sails and spare oilskins.

For safety reasons there are lifelines either side of the deck which are attached to the pulpit at the bow and the pushpit at the stern. Nevertheless, people can still fall overboard so safety equipment *must* be carried.

The backstay has a multiple purchase so that it can be adjusted readily. On the *J24* the backstay goes to the top of the mast, but the forestay does not. So tightening the backstay will put more bend in the mast because the top section will come aft. In strong winds the backstay is used in this way to flatten the mainsail. Tension then has to be applied to the Cunningham to restore the point of maximum draft to the forward third of the sail. If the wind strength is still too much, the crew can reduce the sail area as shown later.

26

23

Continued from
opposite page
16 Topping lift
17 Sail cover
18 Backstay
19 Forestay
20 Shrouds
21 Lower
shrouds
22 Spreader
23 Hounds
24 Topsides
25 Waterline
26 Masthead
wind
indicator

20

22

21

19

18

3

1

24

25

10

Using the winches

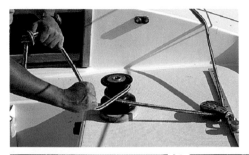

Left and below: the correct method. The left hand controls the sheet, the right hand wraps it round. Insert the handle and wind with the left hand.

It is very important that the winches are used properly. Good winch work makes boat handling so much easier. Bad winch work can cause emergencies or personal injury. Here, the jib sheet is wound onto the winch correctly.

Hold the jib sheet with your left hand and pull. Reach forward with your right hand so that you can grasp the sheet and wrap it clockwise round the winch. Pull in with both hands but never wrap a sheet around your hand. (A sudden gust may overpower you, you will not be able to unwrap the sheet, and your hand will be dragged into the jib pulley block with painful consequences.) If your timing has been good during a tack, you may be able to pull the sheet all the way in but, if you require extra power, use the winch handle.

Right and far right: the mainsheet is taken round pulley blocks mounted at the end of the boom. Here you see a demonstration of how to pull the sheet in while still holding the tiller. You cannot go hand over hand so you grip the rope with your tiller hand then reach down and grasp the rope. Finally, pull up and grip again with your tiller hand.

Most winches have two speeds. Turn the handle one way for winding in quickly, and then, when it gets harder, reverse the direction to bring in the last part of the sheet. You will need the handle to fine tune the jib when it is full of wind. To ease the sheet, using your hand as a break, place it on the sheet around the winch to prevent jerking.

In a light boat, one person works the sheet winches. But on large boats the job is normally split so that one person holds the sheet and the other winds the winch. You should carry a spare winch handle because, for some unaccountable reason, handles do tend to disappear overboard into the sea!

The pictures (*right*) show some common errors. I.e. to release a riding turn is not easy.

Do not have your hand too close to winch. You could damage a finger.

Do not wind the sheet the wrong way. It is always wound round clockwise. It helps to paint an arrow on the winch.

You should never hold a sheet in front of a winch. It is dangerous and can cause a riding turn.

Do not use too many turns as this also can cause a riding turn.

A riding turn. The sheet is jammed on the winch.

Tacking

A cruiser takes much more time and room to manoeuvre. The helmsman needs to be extremely sensitive to the feel of the boat and to use the helm smoothly with a steady pressure. He should not put the helm over too far or too fast. In these pictures the actions of the helmsman and crew are seen from on board.

The helmsman has checked to see that there is room to tack and warned the jib sheet hand to prepare to tack. She prepares by winding the windward jib sheet around the winch. He puts the helm down gently (1). She moves across the

During the tack the two other crew members have been making use of their weight to carry out a manoeuvre known as 'roll tacking'. This is an advanced technique which helps speed up the tack and give an increased boost to the wind in the sails. The pictures in this sequence show how this is done.

The helmsman has told them to prepare to tack (6). He shouts 'lee oh!' and heads up into the wind (7). The crew are leaning out to make the boat roll into the tack. Note that the jib is still on its original side, which helps to blow the bow round (8). The consequence of staying to leeward is that the crew have to move across

boat as it starts to go head to wind and unwinds what was the leeward jib sheet from the winch. She has the other jib sheet in her left hand (2). The main boom moves across and she starts to pull in the leeward jib sheet on the new tack, while he keeps the helm over. Note that he never puts it over too far and stands up to move across the boat (3). Still standing to get a better view, the helmsman changes steering hands behind his back (4). Helmsman and jib sheet hand trim the sails and settle down to sailing on the new tack (5).

very quickly. One goes round the front of the mast. The other pulls himself under the boom (9). They climb back into position on the rail in time to augment the boat's roll in the other direction. This helps it to bear away and complete the tack more quickly. The tack is now complete (10).

Gybing

The helmsman *must* ensure that no-one is standing near the boom when gybing. The result of being hit by it could be a serious injury, man overboard or both. This could happen if the boat gybes unexpectedly, because the wind suddenly gets to the back side of the sail and whips it over. The helmsman must stay alert. He should watch the masthead wind indicator, the telltales on the sail and the ripples on the water. If these indicate that he is sailing by the lee, he should either alter course by luffing up or carry out a properly executed gybe rather than be surprised by an involuntary one.

1 The helmsman checks to make sure there is sufficient room to gybe and tells the crew: 'stand by to gybe!'.

2 The helmsman stands up and grabs hold of the mainsheet close to the boom. The jib sheet hand has already put the windward sheet round the winch. The crew stay on the windward side, their weight helping the boat to turn.

3 The helmsman shouts 'gybe oh!', moves the helm over and pulls the boom in with the mainsheet. The crew starts to duck.

4 You can see why the crew have to duck. The boom is low on this boat. But it is short enough to pass in front of the helmsman so he can remain standing.

5 The jib sheet hand pulls in the jib sheet as she moves across. Notice how the crew all move across together. The helmsman is still steering with his right hand.

6 The helmsman passes the tiller extension to his left hand.

4

5

In a large cruiser, the boom is very heavy and the forces in the sail can be considerable, so a different technique is used to reduce the weight of wind in the boom when it comes over. After the command 'stand by to gybe', the first step is to pull on the main sheet until it is amidships. The helm is then pulled over. As soon as the wind pressure switches to the other side, the main sheet hand pays out the sheet slowly – not letting it run *through* his hands but using a hand over hand technique – so that the boom swings out smoothly.

Above: the helms-man grasps all the parts of the main-sheet, and the crew has the jib sheet round the winch and is ready to pull it in.

Below: make sure nobody is standing where they could be hit by the boom.

6

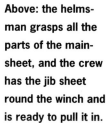

Spinnaker: hoisting and lowering

Right: the foredeck hand releases the pole uphaul from the bottom of the mast and lifts up the inboard end of the pole.

Left: the crew pull on the uphaul and cleat it when the pole is horizontal. The downhaul is also cleated to stop the pole from rising. You can see the uphaul and downhaul, and the spinnaker guy (coloured blue) threaded through the end of the pole. The jib sheets (coloured red) have to lie over the top of the pole. The foredeck hand makes a final check to see that the lines are untwisted and leading correctly.

1 The pole is up. At the command 'hoist', the foredeck hand pulls on the spinnaker halyard, the cockpit crew pulls the spinnaker guy which draws the spinnaker clew forwards.
2 The spinnaker is nearly up and the clew has been pulled round as far as the end of the spinnaker pole.

3 With the spinnaker raised, the foredeck hand cleats the spinnaker halyard and the crew releases the jib halyard.
4 The foredeck hand moves to the bow and pulls the jib right down.

On a cruiser, the tasks required to hoist and lower the spinnaker are spread amongst the crew, so good planning and coordination are required to ensure that everyone knows in advance what they have to do.

The spinnaker pole is stowed on the deck of the *J24*. It has a topping lift to pull it up and a downhaul to prevent it from rising too high. Both these lines are permanently attached and lead from the mast back to the cockpit so that they can be adjusted from there. The uphaul is kept tidy by clipping it to the bottom of the mast. The jib sheets pass over the pole when it is not in use and lies stowed on deck.

The procedure for hoisting the spinnaker starts with preparing the pole for use. The pole will go up on the opposite side to the main boom. The foredeck hand has to check that the spinnaker guy is clipped through the hook at the end. He also checks that nothing is likely to become tangled. For example, the spinnaker, must be packed without any twists in it, and is ready to come out of the cabin hatch. Problems are best dealt with before they arise. It is hard to untwist the spinnaker when it is flapping around halfway up the mast.

5 The crew pulls the spinnaker guy round into position using the winch and cleats it. The spinnaker trimmer stands and starts to adjust it.

6 When dropping the spinnaker the procedure is reversed: the cockpit crew hoists the jib and the foredeck hand uncleats the halyard.

7 The foredeck hand releases the halyard and the crew gather the spinnaker in. The jib trimmer adjusts the jib sheet.

8 The foredeck hand pays out the halyard, hand over hand, while two crew members bundle it into the cabin. The sail will be tidied up afterwards.

Spinnaker reaching

If a hull is very narrow, like those of a catamaran, it makes very little wash because it slices through the water. But as a keel boat increases its speed, its bow wave becomes longer and deeper. In the picture *below* two crests are clearly visible. The forward crest stays just behind the bow. The aft one moves further back as the speed increases. The faster the speed of the boat, the further apart the two crests move. But once the aft crest reaches the stern of the boat it can go no further. So there is a theoretical maximum speed beyond which a boat normally cannot go.

But some cruisers are designed to be light enough to rise over their bow waves and plane like a dinghy. A *J24* is in its element on a fast spinnaker reach. The spinnaker is set high to encourage the bow to lift. Crew weight is

Below: here the boat is making a large bow wave and is low in the water. It is close to its maximum displacement speed.

Above: here the boat has broken through its own bow wave and is planing just like a dinghy.

moved aft for the same reason and has the added bonus of keeping the rudder in the water to maintain control. The crew members have to keep the boat upright because too much heel can cause a broach, which is when the boat turns sharply into the wind regardless of how much rudder correction you try to apply. If this happens release the spinnaker sheet completely, which should take the force off the spinnaker.

Never release the guy otherwise you will completely lose control of the spinnaker.

If overpowered by the wind force the helmsman can also bear away, which will reduce the apparent wind, or he can release the mainsheet. In case this is insufficient, a crew member should have the kicking strap in his hand, ready to release it further to reduce the wind force in the mainsail.

Below: the crew are enjoying the ride.

Man overboard drill

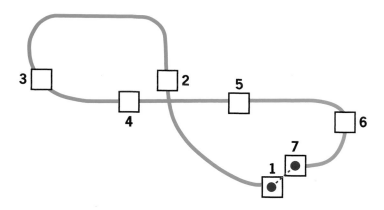

If you or a member of your crew fall overboard from a cruiser it is a serious situation. It is not easy to pick up anyone in calm seas and good visibility. At night, or in a gale, it is very difficult indeed. It is imperative, therefore, that you and your crew learn the correct rescue drill and that you practise it, as often as you can and at least twice a season.

Whoever sees the accident must shout 'Man overboard!' loud enough to bring everyone on deck. But he must *NOT* take his eyes off the man in the water and he must keep pointing at him. Someone must throw out a lifebelt immediately, if possible to windward of the man so it drifts down on him. Do not hit him on the head. A dan buoy should be attached to the lifebelt. If it is not, throw it in separately.

The quickest way to turn is to gybe, but this could damage the boat. A safer way is to take your time and tack, even though the turning circle will be greater.

It is also better to return upwind of the man in the water, because you can then drift down onto him and your boat will shield him from the wind and create a smoother patch of water for the rescue. Picking up a man out of the water into a high sided boat is extremely difficult. If manpower is not enough to haul him back on board, use a spare halyard for him to hang on to and winch him aboard.

When you practise the rescue drill, take your time or you will find it difficult to get back in position. Each crew member should take turns to steer. In a real emergency it may well be the skipper who goes overboard.

This sequence shows the crew practising with a mooring buoy: the buoy is thrown overboard and there is a shout of 'Man overboard'. Someone is told to act as spotter. The helmsman steers onto a reach and the sails are trimmed accordingly. They wait for some 20 seconds before tacking. This gives them room to make a turn. They then head back on the broad reach. The helmsman has then to judge very carefully the point to bring the boat up into the wind so that it slows down and stops right by the buoy. The worst thing is to approach too fast because you will overshoot and have to repeat the whole process, and if speed is not totally under control you could run down the person you are rescuing.

4
The numbers on the illustrations are mirrored in the diagram (above, left) showing the sequence of the rescue manoeuvre.

Reducing sail

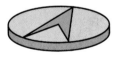

Above: the sail is fully up.

In strong winds, you must reduce the sail area. This can be done either by putting up a smaller jib or by reducing the mainsail's size, an action called reefing. If a smaller jib is hoisted, and the mainsail stays the same, the rig's centre of effort will change and so will the boat's balance. Experiment to find out the best combination for your boat.

Some boats have large, light-wind jibs known as genoas. These would normally be changed first if the wind increases as a smaller sail is easier to handle and is made out of a stronger cloth. To change a foresail you drop it first, then unclip it from the forestay, detach it from the jib sheets, and put it away before carrying out these actions in reverse order to hoist a new sail. On some racing boats it is possible to set the new sail before the old one is dropped thus minimising any loss of speed.

The next step is to reef the mainsail. The picture sequence shows how this is done. The foredeck hand goes to the mast and prepares to pull the sail down. One of the crew takes the halyard off the winch (1). He pulls down on the luff of the sail, and the halyard is released a little. The helmsman eases the mainsheet (2). The foredeck hand hooks the cringle in the sail over the reefing hook on the boom (3). One crew member puts the halyard round the winch, while another puts the handle in the winch and winds (4). A crew member cleats the halyard. The foredeck hand pulls the reefing line, which runs inside the boom to the leech of the sail. The helmsman then gives it a tweak to help it

3

4

Below: the sail has been reefed and is reduced in size.

6

7

down (5). The foredeck hand cleats the reefing line. The helmsman pulls the mainsheet in again (6). Reefing the mainsail completed (7). This method is called slab reefing but roller reefing, rolling the mainsail round the boom, is also commonly adopted. Note that throughout the manoeuvre the jib stays filled with wind so the boat never stops.

Right: the jib has been lowered. The hanks are unclipped from the forestay so that the jib can be replaced.

Anchoring

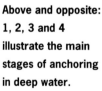

Above and opposite: 1, 2, 3 and 4 illustrate the main stages of anchoring in deep water.

When anchoring, pick a suitable spot where there is enough room for the boat to swing round on its anchor chain without hitting anything and where you are sheltered from wind and waves. It must be out of the main channel and well away from any shore to leeward, or a lee shore as it is called. This is where you will finish up if the anchor does not hold the boat. If your anchor fails, you need space to deal with the problem.

Tides and currents are explained later, but, in order to anchor in a safe spot, you have to work out the depth of water and you must be aware of the state of the tide. In particular beware of a falling tide. It would be extremely embarrassing to anchor in a good depth of water, only to find yourself high and dry after lunch. On the other hand, the water may be so deep that you do not have enough chain. It needs to be at least three times the maximum depth of water, preferably more, and must be

marked so that you know the length that has been put out. You also need to know the best type of anchor for the sea bottom in the area you normally sail in.

Sometimes boats lie with their bows pointing into the wind, sometimes pointing into the tide, and sometimes between the two. It depends on the relative strengths of these two factors, but normally the tide dominates. The best clue is boats already anchored. You must then approach your chosen spot in the direction you expect your boat to lie.

The picture sequence shows a nice gentle approach into the wind with no tide. The crew has released the jib halyard and the foredeck hand has pulled the jib down. The foredeck hand prepares the chain. He takes the anchor forwards, out through the bow fairlead and brings it back over the pulpit. He is now ready to throw it over. The helmsman picks his spot and judges how far past it to go before heading

3

up into the wind. He has to sail beyond his chosen spot because he has to allow for the boat to drift backwards until the anchor takes hold (1). As the boat stops, the foredeck hand throws the anchor into the water clear of the bow (2). The chain is vertical, indicating that the anchor is directly below, but it is still running free. The crew holds the main boom out so the boat starts to sail backwards. The idea is to jerk the chain when it becomes taut. This helps the anchor to dig in. However, do not do this if the bottom is very muddy as the anchor may get stuck (3). The chain lying at a good angle, suggests that the anchor is holding. When the boat has settled, the skipper checks the anchor is not dragging by working out a transit (4), see page 140. He should check the boat's position again after a few minutes.

4

Coming alongside

When coming alongside, it is important that you plan your approach in advance. Explain to the crew exactly what you propose to do and allot a job to each.

Check the direction and the strength of both the wind and the tide. Unless you have a strong tide running against you, the only way you are going to be able to slow down when under sail – apart from hitting something! – is to head into the wind. Make sure you have plenty of room to do this. If the tide is running with you, it is almost impossible to stop dead on a mark. So it is preferable to approach against the tide.

You must adapt your approach to the prevailing conditions. The method shown in this sequence is but one example of how it is done and only shows the general principles.

Approaching your berth

1 Two fenders have been put out beforehand to protect the topsides of the boat against any damage from bumping. The jib has been dropped to reduce speed and doing this also improves the helmsman's view.

The bow hand has taken the bow rope forwards, passed it through the fairlead and back over the pulpit so that it will lie and hold correctly when taken ashore.

2 The helmsman reduces the boat's speed by pointing head to wind.

3 The boat slows down. If it is still moving too fast, back the mainsail to create a braking effect.

4 As soon as the bow reaches the post, the bow hand takes a turn around it with the rope. The mainsail is dropped. The boat is now secure and can be moored up properly. It is secured with two mooring lines, the bow rope and the stern rope, and two lines known as springs. Do not leave lines across the quay or pontoon because people may trip over them.

The sequence for tying up is as follows:

5 Tie a clove hitch around round post.

6 Bring the line back to the centre of the boat to form a spring.

7 Do the same at the stern.

8 Move the traveller to one side for easier access to the cabin. Hang the mainsheet up to dry. Tie the rudder in a central position so that the boat does not try to turn.

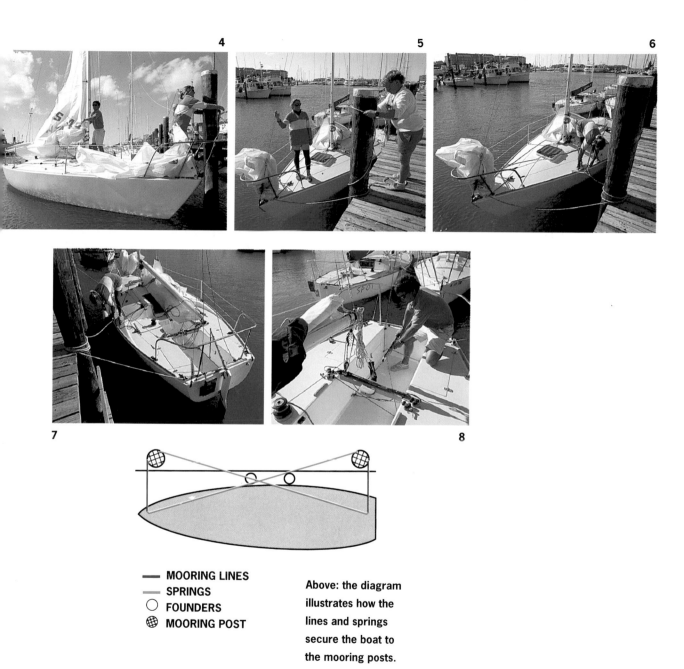

4

5

6

7

8

— MOORING LINES
— SPRINGS
○ FOUNDERS
⊕ MOORING POST

Above: the diagram
illustrates how the
lines and springs
secure the boat to
the mooring posts.

Cruiser safety equipment

A cruiser must be equipped with lifejackets for all the crew. Ordinary ones are bulky so inflatable ones are also manufactured which can be inflated either by mouth or automatically with a CO_2 bottle. The crew must also have a harness each or wear a sailing jacket to which lifelines can be attached. These have quick release hooks which can be hooked on to secure parts like the pulpit when on deck. In heavy weather everyone must wear a harness or a lifejacket, or both, and one or both must be used by all crew members during a night passage whatever the conditions.

Equipment for man overboard emergencies must include at least one horse-shoe lifebelt with an automatic light, whistle, a dye marker, and a dan buoy which can be thrown to mark the spot. This must be at least 2 metres tall and be equipped with a drogue to stop it drifting away from the man in the water. Keep them all close to the helmsman, ready for instant use.

Other safety equipment should include white and red flares. During a night passage white flares should be at hand if the helmsman needs to draw a ship's attention to his yacht. Red flares are lit in distress to summon help

KEY
1 **Life jacket**
2 **Inflatable life jacket**
3 **Harness**
4 **Sailing jacket**
5 **Horse-shoe life belt**
6 **Automatic light**
7 **Dan buoy**
8 **Drogue**
9 **Flares**

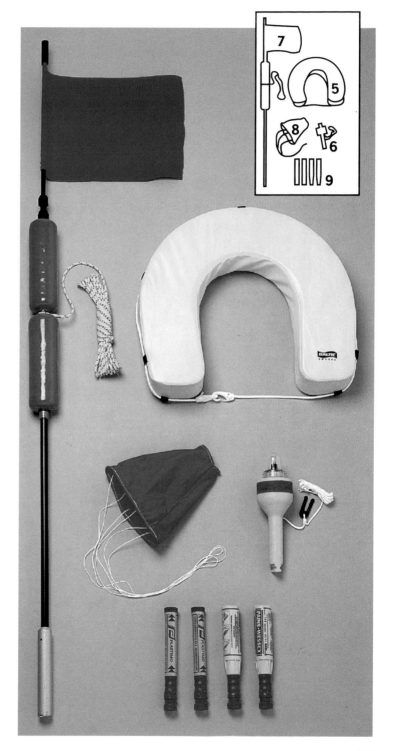

from the Coastguard or a lifeboat. Orange smoke flares perform the same function and are more visible in bright daylight.

A cruiser venturing off-shore is well advised to carry a properly serviced inflatable life-raft. Other items worth carrying are a spare anchor, an emergency tiller, some provision for repairing leaks in the hull, and a spare bilge pump. A radar reflector will ensure your craft shows up clearly on the sets of nearby ships, and a VHF ship-to-shore radio is an invaluable extra safety item, which all members of the crew should be able to operate.

THE SAILBOARD
How the sailboard works

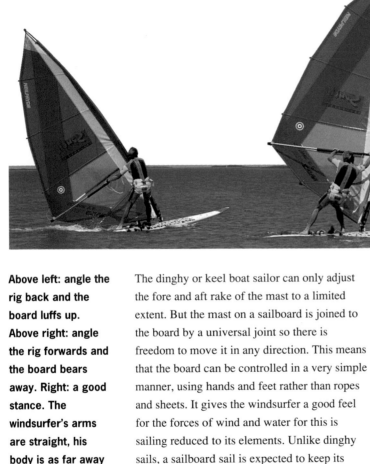

Above left: angle the rig back and the board luffs up. Above right: angle the rig forwards and the board bears away. Right: a good stance. The windsurfer's arms are straight, his body is as far away from the sail as possible to minimise turbulence. The mast is pulled slightly to windward which puts the sail's centre of effort over the centre line of the sailboard.

The dinghy or keel boat sailor can only adjust the fore and aft rake of the mast to a limited extent. But the mast on a sailboard is joined to the board by a universal joint so there is freedom to move it in any direction. This means that the board can be controlled in a very simple manner, using hands and feet rather than ropes and sheets. It gives the windsurfer a good feel for the forces of wind and water for this is sailing reduced to its elements. Unlike dinghy sails, a sailboard sail is expected to keep its shape and it is hard to adjust it on the water. Monofilm is a popular material for sailboard sails because it resists stretch and holds its shape. It also repels water making it easier to pull up and its transparency gives the windsurfer good visibility. But it rips easily and has to be handled and stored with great care.

The sailboard is rigged by passing the mast inside a tube sewn into the front of the sail. The tope of the tube is sealed and covered with a reinforcement where the top of the mast presses onto it. The luff of the sail can then be tensioned by pulling down at the tack using a system of pulleys known as the downhaul.

The boom is double-sided, is shaped like a wishbone, and is attached to the mast at the front. At the other end there is a line which runs to the clew of the sail. This is called the outhaul. A rope suspended from the front of the boom, called the uphaul, is used for pulling the rig out of the water.

The sailboard illustrated on these pages has a pivoting daggerboard – the equivalent of a centreboard – which the windsurfer adjusts by pushing it with his foot. Normally, it is lowered when sailing to windward and raised completely when sailing downwind.

Steering is achieved by moving the rig and altering the angle of the board in the water. A small fixed fin at the stern called the skeg (not a rudder) is essential to keep the board sailing in a straight line.

The windsurfer faces the sail and holds the wishbone boom with both hands. The front hand is known as the mast hand because it controls the rake of the mast. The back hand is known as the sheet hand because, by moving the sail across the board, it controls (like a main sheet in a dinghy) the angle of the sail. In the *picture on the left* lines are fixed to the boom and pass round a hook on his harness. This takes the strain off his arms. The hook is pointing downwards – one pull with his arms to bring the boom closer and the line drops out of the hook and he can detach himself easily.

In a gust the windsurfer can spill wind from the sail by sheeting out with his back hand. Alternatively, he can lower his body and pull the sail over his head by putting more weight on the harness lines. The power in the sail will be reduced, because it presents a smaller projected area to the wind.

Above: the disadvantage of windsurfing is that if you fall off you have to climb back on again, and then pull the sail back out of the water.

Above: a technique called 'water starting' has been developed which uses the wind to pull you out of the water. Right: the windsurfer has nearly reached his normal sailing position as the board starts to move off.

Tacking and gybing

Above: the gybe. Holding the sail over the windward side causes the wind to push the board round. The turn is helped by standing towards the back and tipping the board to windward.

In most sailing craft the centre of effort is an imaginary point. On a sailboard you can actually find the position of the centre of effort in the sail. Place your hands on the boom so that there is equal pressure on each arm. Then move your hands towards each other keeping even pressure on your arms. Note where your thumbs meet. The sail feels balanced because you are holding it in line with the centre of effort. If you moved your hands back the front of the sail would move away from you. Conversely, if you moved your hands forwards the back of the sail would move away from you. With your hands comfortably balanced on the boom you can steer by moving the rig and

therefore the centre of effort. Move it forwards and the board turns away from the wind; move it backwards and the board turns into the wind – just as a dinghy can be steered by sheeting in one sail or another. But you can also move the sail to one side and the board will turn to the other. To help it turn you can press down on the outer side. So the principles of sailing which have been demonstrated with the dinghy without a rudder (on pages 62-65) are exactly the same ones used by the windsurfer.

The sequence of pictures here show how a windsurfer can be taken through all the basic sailing manoeuvres purely by moving the sail.

Starting from a neutral position, the

windsurfer rakes the mast back and the board luffs up onto a close hauled course (1). Keeping the mast back, the board turns towards the wind. He steps forwards and places one foot in front of the mast (2). He steps round the front of the mast and faces the sail on the other side (3). He places his hand on the boom and keeps the sail forwards so that the board continues to turn (4). He has completed the tack and is sailing close hauled on the port tack (5). He moves the sail forwards which causes the board to bear away onto a reach (6). He now brings the mast well forwards, and the board bears away onto a broad reach (7). He moves his weight back on the board which increases the turning effect of

the sail (8). He brings the sail forwards and to the left and the board turns on to a running course. He is facing forwards, looking ahead through the window in the sail (9). He lets go with his right hand, still holding the mast up with his left, and the sail swings round in front of him. He has completed a gybe (10). He then moves his hands to the new side of the boom, adjusts the sail, and the board sails in a straight line on the starboard tack (11).

Above: the tack. The windsurfer has turned the board into the wind by holding the sail back. He completes the turn by bringing the sail forwards to bring the board onto its new course.

High speed windsurfing

In strong winds the windsurfer uses a smaller sail and a shorter board. By leaning the sail towards the wind, the windsurfer is able to pull down on the boom. This takes the weight off the feet which allows them to slip into the straps at the back of the board. Using the harness, the weight is directed down through the mast foot. The board is now planing on its aft sections and the skeg ensures that the sailboard tracks in a straight line.

When sailing at speed a different technique is used for steering the board. By altering the pressure on the feet in the footstraps the windsurfer can bank it to one side or the other. This is known as foot steering. To turn round, one always gybes. The dynamic version is the carve gybe when the windsurfer removes the front foot from the straps and banks the board over hard by pressing on the edge. When properly executed the board keeps planing all the way round.

Sailboards are the fastest sailing craft, and the sensation of handling them at speed is so exciting that even apparently sane individuals

Above left: the sailboard at speed. Far left: a successful carve gybe. Above: the speed sailor uses a very small board and wears a helmet for protection.

drop everything and rush to the beach when the wind is strong. But even though it is fun, safety should not be forgotten.

SAFETY NOTE: never go windsurfing without someone being alert to rescue you. *Beware of offshore winds*: if something breaks, or you become tired, you may find it impossible to get back. Boards are very difficult to see when the rig is lying in the water, so make sure someone always knows where you are.

Speed trials are a form of sailing where the craft are timed over a measured distance between two points. The highest speeds are attained by windsurfers and the world record is constantly being broken. In the picture the speed sailor has the sail pulled in tight even though sailing on a reach. This is because the speed has brought the apparent wind well ahead. Note that the sail is pulled back so that the wind cannot escape below it.

SEAMANSHIP AND NAVIGATION
Tides and currents

Tide is the vertical rise and fall of the level of the sea. In some parts of the world the tide is not significant, but in others the difference between high and low water is considerable. When the level is rising or falling in an estuary, water is flowing in or out. Sometimes the tidal flow is very strong indeed which will dictate the way you have to sail your boat. In order to navigate safely, a yachtsman needs to know the height of the tide, and the strength and direction of the current which it causes.

Beware of falling tides!

Tides are caused by gravitational pull, principally the moon's. The Earth revolves every 24 hours, but in that time the moon has moved ahead in its orbit round the earth, so it passes over the same spot on earth every 24 hours and 50 minutes. During this time there are two high tides, so each one is about 12 hours and 25 minutes later than the previous one. This figure is approximate because variations occur. Accurate timings can be obtained from tide tables which also give the height of the tide at high and low water. They are widely available. Their times are Greenwich Mean Time so allow for Summer Time.

The gravitational pull of the sun also affects the tides, but to a lesser extent. When it is in line with the moon (New Moon and Full Moon), its gravitational pull adds to the moon's gravitational pull. This has a greater effect on the tides and makes them both higher and lower than normal. These are known as Spring Tides and they vary in intensity through the year.

SPRING TIDE

Moon

Earth

Sun

NEAP TIDE

Moon

Sun   Earth

Above: when the sun and moon are in line Spring Tides occur; and when they are at 90 degrees Neap Tides occur.

During the equinox (March and September), when the sun lies exactly over the equator, they are exceptionally strong. When the gravitational pull is at its least (Half Moon) the tides are known as Neap Tides. Tides alternate weekly – if there are Spring Tides one weekend, the next weekend there will be Neaps.

The height of the tides can also be affected by barometric pressure; with less air pressure above it, the water level will rise. Also, strong winds can move the surface of the water and cause a build-up of the water level. So tidal predictions are only approximate.

It is helpful to remember that the state of the tide always recurs at the same time in the same place. For example, whenever high water at Cowes is at midday it is always Spring Tides; and whenever it is low water at that time it is always Neap Tides.

The current is the flow of water, and it depends on the amount of rise and fall of tide. The greater the difference in its height the stronger the current. The current slows down as it approaches high or low water, reverses itself when these occur, and reaches its maximum strength at half tide. This can be expressed as the rule of Twelfths:

THE RISE AND FALL OF TIDE IS:
1/12 of Range in First Hour
2/12 of Range in Second Hour
3/12 of Range in Third Hour
3/12 of Range in Fourth Hour
2/12 of Range in Fifth Hour
1/12 of Range in Sixth Hour

The tidal flow, unlike the direction of the wind, is described in terms of the direction it is heading. Thus a southerly wind blows from the south, but a southerly tide flows towards the south. The predicted flows can be found in a Tidal Stream Atlas, but these are not always correct, so it pays to learn how to observe some of the outward signs of the tide's strength and direction:

1 A navigation buoy leans away from the direction of the tide as it pulls on its chain, but moored sailing boats tend to point into the tide.
2 In a tidal river estuary, the current is the water flow out of the river combined with the tidal flow. One reverses, the other does not.
3 The strongest tidal flow in an estuary is in the channel. The weakest is in the shallows.
4 The tide often changes either side of a channel first. So at high tide, in the channel the water will still be flowing in, but will have turned and started to flow out in the shallows.
5 The tide is strongest where a channel is at its narrowest.
6 The tide is very strong round headlands. It can create short sharp waves caused by the rapid movement of the water. These are called tide rips. Often there are eddies downstream of headlands.
7 If the wind is blowing in the opposite direction to the tide, the waves will have sharp crests. When it is blowing in the same direction, the crests are much smoother. So you can often tell the tidal direction by the state of the sea.

The weather

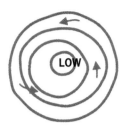

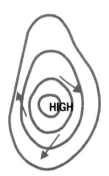

Top: the wind bends towards a low pressure area. Above: the wind moves away from a 'high'. You can remember the direction of the wind if you stand with your back to it; the low pressure is on your left side.

Understanding why the weather changes and how it does so is always useful and may give you the edge over your opponents when racing or enable you to avoid a storm. On these pages, the examples given relate to wind behaviour in the northern hemisphere.

The air in the atmosphere varies in temperature and pressure. If it did not, our weather would not change. Basically, the sun warms the air more at the equator than at the poles. So, in theory, to maintain thermal balance, the warm air flows towards the poles and is replaced by cold air in the opposite direction. However, the actual flow pattern of these air streams is extremely complex. Air masses of different temperatures move in all directions over the globe, baffling even the meteorologists at times.

Warm air is less dense than cold air, so it weighs less and therefore exerts less pressure on the earth's surface. Thus low pressure is associated with warm air and high pressure with cold air. Pressure is measured by a barometer and meteorologists draw maps with lines of equal pressure which are called isobars.

The difference in pressure between air masses causes air to flow from high pressure areas to low pressure ones. However, due to the rotation of the earth, the wind does not flow in straight lines but tends to follow the isobars. In the northern hemisphere, the wind flows anti-clockwise round a 'low' and clockwise round a 'high'. In the southern hemisphere it flows the other way round.

The earth causes frictional resistance to the passage of air. This bends the wind direction towards the centre of a low pressure area and away from the centre of a high one. In both cases the effect is to bend the wind anti-clockwise. Frictional resistance is at its greatest

at ground level so the direction of the wind changes according to the height it is blowing above the ground. Note the blue arrows on the diagram.

Air temperature decreases with height, which is why it is always cooler at the top of a mountain. So a mass of air which is warmer than its surroundings will rise, but as it rises it quickly cools until its temperature is equal to the surrounding air. If it passes over the sea, it picks up moisture from evaporation off the sea. As it cools, it cannot retain as much moisture. Therefore water is released in the form of clouds and this often leads to rain. Conversely, high pressure gives fine weather because the descending cold air, as it warms up, is able to retain more moisture.

When warm and cold airstreams meet there is generally a well-defined boundary between them. But sometimes some of the warm air

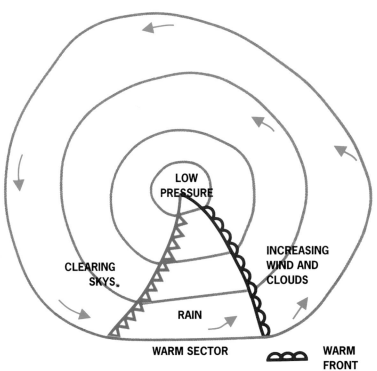

Above: the diagram illustrates the characteristics of a depression.

intrudes into the cold portion. The cold air circulates around the concentration of warm air which in turn grows into a wave shape and a depression is formed. Even a mild depression brings wind and it always causes a change in wind direction. The boundary line between warm and cold air is known as a front.

The area of warm air within a depression is marked by a warm front as the warm air approaches, and a cold front as the cold air marks the end of a sector. Eventually the two fronts come together as the warm air is squeezed upwards and out of the depression. This signals the end of the low pressure area. Notice how the wind veers sharply as each front passes – 'veered' is the technical name for a clockwise wind shift, 'backed' is an anti-clockwise one.

A depression can move slowly. But if you are patient you should notice the following sequence of events when the centre of a depression passes to the north of you:

1 Falling barometer readings.
2 Appearance of thin high cloud.
3 Thickening cloud.
4 Wind increases steadily but does not become gusty. Visibility decreases and heavy rain starts to fall.
5 As the warm front passes over, the rain almost stops, the barometer settles, and the wind veers.
6 As the cold front arrives, there are heavy showers accompanied by strong gusts. This is in contrast to the warm front, where winds are strong but remain steady.
7 As the cold front moves away, the wind veers, the pressure rises, and clouds disperse.

If the depression passes to the south of you, the effects are less extreme and the wind does not change direction so sharply.

Local wind effects

Winds are caused by weather systems which extend over hundreds of miles. But local winds can also blow, and these can be affected by various factors. So it is important to understand how they develop, especially if you are racing anywhere near the shore.

Sea-breezes are the most common local winds. These only occur when the summer sun's rays reach the earth. As the land heats up and cools off more quickly than the sea, it is warmer than the sea in the day and several degrees colder at night.

As the land becomes warmer, it heats the air above it. This rises and is replaced with cold air from above the sea and the result is a sea-breeze. The breeze starts near the beach and, as it develops, it can spread many miles, both out to sea and inland.

Normally, there will also be a wind caused by the pressure differences between isobars. If this is blowing onshore, the sea-breeze will strengthen it. If it is blowing offshore, the sea-breeze can neutralize it. As the sea-breeze strengthens through the day, it can also reverse the wind direction.

Sea-breezes tend to shift during the day in the same direction as the sun. As the sun sets, the sea-breeze disappears and is sometimes replaced by a land-breeze, a gentle zephyr blowing out to sea as the land cools.

Also be aware of how the wind can be affected by the shape of the shore. The frictional resistance of the earth tends to make the wind shift anti-clockwise in relation to that higher up. This effect is more marked over land than water so a wind blowing off the shore veers as it crosses the shore. It will also tend to blow out of river mouths and to funnel between obstructions. When the wind lifts over a solid obstruction it leaves still air to windward,

though trees can be an exception as the wind will penetrate through them.

The good sailor is constantly making adjustments to ensure that his sails are perfectly trimmed to whatever wind is blowing. Do not react too quickly to the wind in your sails, but try to anticipate its strength and direction. A gust normally causes small ripples on the water and this makes the surface appear darker. So keep looking towards the eye of the wind to see if a dark patch is approaching. Other boats sailing there will give you a hint of what wind is coming. Also, glance at the sky: an approaching cloud often brings a gust with it.

You should be aware, too, of the existence of what is called the rhythmic wind shift. This causes a fluctuation in the direction of the wind at regular intervals say every five minutes or so,

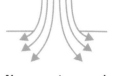

Above: gusts caused by air spreading out as it hits the water.

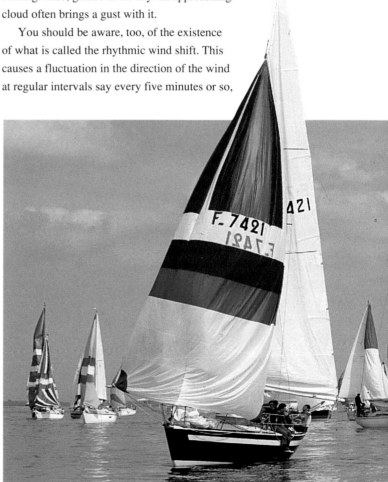

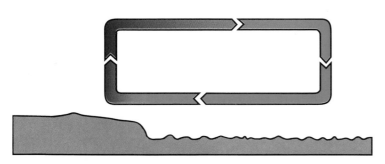

but it does not necessarily cause a change in its strength and speed.

A windshift that brings the wind direction further aft when you are sailing close hauled is known as a lift. This means you can point higher than before, so it pays to keep on sailing. A windshift that brings the wind direction further ahead is known as a header. You cannot point as high so if your course is into the eye of the wind it is better to go about as you will able to point higher on the other tack. If you are racing, it is essential to do so.

Above: circulation is maintained by warm air in the upper atmosphere returning seaward and cooling.

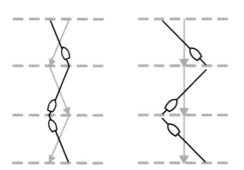

Far left: the boat has improved its tacking angle by going about when the wind shifts.

Left: in a steady wind, the boat can only tack through 90 degrees. Below: waiting for the wind.

Rules of the road

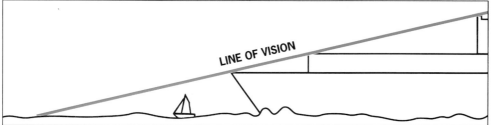

LINE OF VISION

Left: small craft in 'blind spot' of large vessel.
Diagrams below and right illustrate Rules of the Road.

1

2

The International Regulations for Preventing Collisions at Sea, more commonly known as the Rules of the Road, are a legal framework designed to deal with any given situation when two vessels are close to each other by defining which vessel has the right of way. All sailors must read them. If yours is the right of way vessel, you should hold your course and allow the other vessel to steer round you. Do not try to take avoiding action as well, or confusion may result. It is helpful if the giving way vessel makes an early and decisive alteration of course as this indicates to the skipper of the right of way vessel that he has been seen.

The one part of the Rules of the Road that most people know about is that 'power gives way to sail'. In fact, this is a dangerous generalisation which in these days of super tankers has many exceptions. Do not try to interpret it too literally with commercial ships. In estuaries and harbours, they are often constrained by their depth. Remember, too, that

they need much deeper water than you do; that they have so much momentum that they can take miles to respond to the helm or to slow down; and that the captain cannot see small boats under his bow and they can be difficult to see on radar. So keep out of the way of large ships in confined waters. The best way of doing this is to keep out of the shipping channels. If you have to cross them do so as quickly and as obviously as possible.

In open water, ships generally avoid a sailing boat if it has been seen, but it is best to keep well away from commercial traffic. A large ship obstructs your wind and then gives you a rough ride with its heavy bow wave. If you must sail close, it is safer to pass astern of a ship rather than ahead.

When two boats are close to one another, remember, these key Rules of the Road:

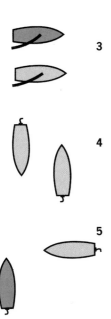

1 The overtaking boat keeps clear.

2 The sailing boat on port tack keeps clear of the one on starboard.

3 The windward sailing boat keeps clear of the leeward one.

4 When two power boats – or sailing boats with their engines running – are approaching each other, they should pass on each other's port side. This means that all vessels must move up and down the right side of a channel or river.

5 When two power boats - or sailing boats with their engines running - are crossing each other, the one with the other on its starboard side must keep clear.

And finally, of course, but not illustrated in the diagrams is where, subject to its ability to manoeuvre, a powered vessel gives way to one under sail. But make sure you have been seen before you assume you are in the clear.

139

Transits and how to use them

Right: as long as the posts are in line from your vantage point, you are on the dotted line.

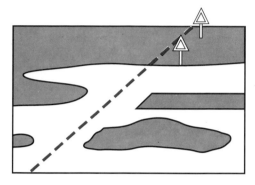

Below: if you are heading for a buoy, find a landmark on the shore. As you approach, the buoy should keep the same relationship with the landmark. If the buoy moves to the right, you should steer to the right. If the buoy moves to the left, you should steer to the left.

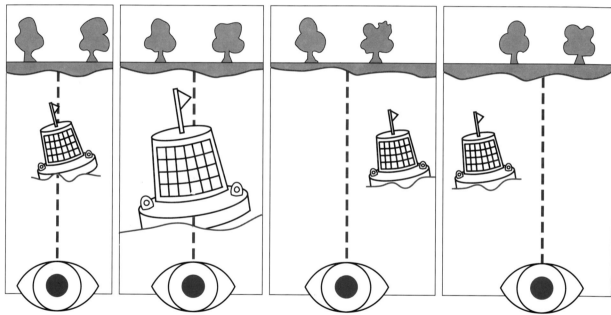

Even though the top boat is moving faster than the other one, the compass bearing of each boat from the other does not change. They are on a collision course.

When two posts are in line vertically, they are said to be in transit. Some harbours have two beacons strategically placed, so that if you keep them in line you avoid any hazards and make a safe passage into port. They are marked on nautical charts and the compass bearing is given as well.

You can use this principle to steer a straight course across a tidal channel or a river to a buoy on the other side. If there is a strong tide taking you to port it is difficult to judge how much to steer to starboard. But if you use a transit, by keeping the buoy stationary in relation to a

Left: the compass is
an essential piece of
equipment when
cruising. This type is
fixed to the boat.

selected object on the land behind it, you will
steer the correct course.

The same principle applies in situations
when a boat is approaching you. If the boat
moves forwards in relation to the background, it
will pass ahead. If it moves backwards, it will
pass behind. This is useful to know when your
courses are crossing and you have to give way.
If you intend to pass ahead of the other yacht,
you must ensure its bow is moving backwards
on the land. However, it is often safer to pass
astern of a yacht with the right of way, so make
sure the stern of the other yacht is moving
forwards against the land. If you are sailing a
boat of some length, it is a wise precaution to
send a crew member up to the bow to sight the
transit from there.

It may be easy to judge the speed of another
boat similar to your own, but to assess
accurately the speed of large ships is another
matter. If the land stays stationary behind a
ship, you are on a collision course and one of
you must do something! The bigger the ship the
more deceptive it can be. For example, though
you may see its bow moving forwards in
relation to the background the stern may not be.
If this is happening, you will hit the stern.

A more reliable method of telling if you are
on a collision course is to take a compass
bearing. Then, having noted it, to take another.
If the bearing does not change, it indicates that
you are on a collision course. The compass
method is used by sailors off-shore and is
invaluable at night.

RACING
Types of racing

At some time or another most sailing people become involved in racing, if only as an informal expression of their competitive instinct. For instance, a cruising skipper who feels that he can sail his boat well, often tests his skill by comparing his speed against a similar boat. So when there is another heading for the same harbour there is often a little friendly competition between the two skippers to see who can get home first.

If you want more than just a race back to the yacht club bar, you can get your sporting excitement by pitting your wits and sailing ability against others in a formally organised race. To do this you will need to join a sailing club which almost certainly runs one or more of the following kinds of races.

Class and One Design Racing

Some classes lay down the parameters, such as overall length and maximum sail area, and allow the boat designer to use his expertise to develop the fastest shape within the rules. These are known as restricted classes.

Other classes have strict rules which allow no room for variation and all the boats are supposed to be identical. This places a premium on the crew's skill in handling the boat. These are called one designs of which both the *470* and the *J24* are examples.

In class racing all the boats start together and the first one over the finishing line is the winner. Olympic races are sailed in one design classes, like the *470*.

Handicap Racing

Each boat is measured against a formula and given a rating. This produces a correction factor which is applied to the time that it takes a yacht to finish the course. The yacht with the lowest

corrected time is the winner. This enables yachts of all sorts and sizes to compete against each other. For example, although the *J24* is a one design class with its own class meetings, it also has a handicap rating. This means that a *J24* can also race against other types of boat in handicap races.

Larger boats are able to race off-shore and these races are held under the Handicap Rules. For example, in the Admirals Cup series, teams of three boats from each country are entered. The boats have to be of difference sizes and therefore have different handicap ratings. So at the finish you will normally see the largest boats crossing the finishing line first. But to finish with a good corrected time they have to be well ahead, because they have the largest handicap penalty.

Match Racing

This is a highly tactical form of racing where only two boats take part. It does not matter how fast you sail as long as you finish before the other fellow. This is the format for the America's Cup.

Team Racing

Carried out between teams of three one design boats, the scope for tactics is enormous, since the objective is to maximise your team's score. The boat in the lead will often stop and wait to help team mates by delaying the opposition. Tactics include obstructing the opponent's wind and advanced use of the racing rules. It is not for beginners.

The only way to learn how to race is to participate. Some lessons and tactics are only learnt by experience and crewing for a competitive skipper is an ideal way to start.

Starting to race

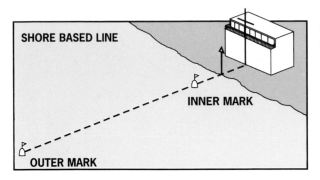

SHORE BASED LINE
INNER MARK
OUTER MARK

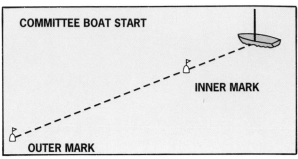

COMMITTEE BOAT START
INNER MARK
OUTER MARK

Above and above right: two methods of starting a race over a line.

ROUNDING TO PORT

ROUNDING TO STARBOARD

Above: the directions for how to round a buoy are usually declared when the course is set.

A race is governed by the written sailing instructions which are issued by the race committee of your sailing club. These explain the course, how the starting line is defined, and which of the racing rules will apply.

The actual course will often not be declared until the last moment, so that the race committee can pick the most suitable one for the weather conditions. The course may be defined by listing buoys in the order you will come to them with instructions on how to round them. If you are instructed to 'round to port' this means you must leave the buoy to port. The buoys that are positioned to mark the course are called racing marks.

The course always includes at least one windward leg. The buoy at the windward end of the course is called the windward mark and the boats approach it while close hauled. At the opposite end of the course is the leeward mark.

Club races are usually started from a point on-shore. The starting line, defined by two transit posts, is the imaginary line connecting these posts extended over the water. A buoy, called the outer limit mark, defines the end of the line and there is also often an inner mark to prevent boats from crowding too close to the shore. These marks do not have to lie directly on the line and often they do not. Their purpose is only to ensure that boats sail between them.

Right top: jostling for position before the start.

This type of line is convenient for the club to operate and it is also easy for competitors to judge the position of the line.

For large fleets a committee boat start is used. Here the line is between the committee boat and an outer limit mark, though sometimes an inner limit mark is laid as well to keep competitors away from the committee boat. It is much harder for competitors to judge this line, although sometimes they can find a transit point on shore to help them. The advantage is that the line can be set directly across the wind so that boats are spread out evenly along it and are not congested at one end. It is normally set well away from the shore so that competitors have plenty of room to manoeuvre.

The club's race committee may use fixed marks and buoys to define a course. The larger fleets lay their own marks. In this case the course is usually based on the Olympic system with rounds alternating between a triangle and a straight windward/leeward loop. On an Olympic course, the first mark is always to windward of the line.

144

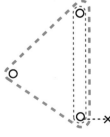

- - -
---- **FIRST LAP**
     SECOND LAP

**Above: laps
alternate between a
triangle and a
windward/leeward
loop.**

You should check the starting sequence actually defined by the sailing instructions because it can vary depending on the rules of the organising club. The starting sequence is communicated to the fleet by means of flags and sound signals (usually guns firing blank cartridges). Normally there will be a preparatory signal 10 minutes before the race when the class flag is raised. At the second preparatory signal the flag P (the Blue Peter) is raised. This indicates that the racing rules are now in force, so you could be penalised for an infringement from this point onwards.

At the starting gun, both flags are lowered and the race is on. At this instant the whole of your boat has to be behind the starting line. The race officers can sight down the line and if any boat has started prematurely a second gun is fired. If the offending boat or boats, and they will usually know who they are, do not return to a position behind the line and restart, they will certainly risk disqualification. If too many boats are over the line a third gun is fired and the race is started again.

Although the penalties for starting prematurely are severe, it is a serious error to start late because you risk being in the wind shadow of the fleet. You will be left to wallow while the leaders race ahead. So, starting is a very critical part of the race.

The racing rules

1

2   WINDWARD

LEEWARD

3

4

T
H
E

S
H
O
R
E

5

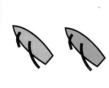

The racing rules are contained in a booklet which is issued by the International Yacht Racing Union and is updated every four years. You may not believe it when you watch a competitive fleet in action, but the rules are framed to ensure fair competition and to prevent collision between yachts.

The rules are complex and it takes time to learn them well enough to use them tactically as the experts do. It is more important to understand the *basic* rules. They cover most of the situations that are likely to occur when racing and are the ones that everyone should learn before starting to race.

If an experienced sailor uses the rules to gain an advantage over you, regard it as a learning experience. You can try it on someone else next time.

The three most basic rules are similar to the Rules of the Road:

1 A boat on the port tack keeps clear of one on the starboard tack.

2 If both boats are on the same tack, the windward one must keep clear.

3 If both boats are on the same tack, the boat clear astern must keep clear of the one ahead.

In a race, where boats are often in close proximity, the following rules also apply:

4 A boat tacking or gybing must keep clear of a boat on a tack. In other words, do not change direction immediately into the path of an oncoming boat.

5 An exception to 4 is the case when a yacht which is ahead and to leeward may be forced to tack to avoid an obstruction such as the shore, or a yacht with the right of way. In these circumstances the helmsman may call out to the other helmsman to give him room to tack. He does this by shouting 'water!' and then the helmsman of the following yacht, for safety reasons, is obliged to make room.

A special rule deals with situations while rounding a mark. If two boats are overlapped (the bow of one overlaps the stern of the one ahead of it) when the leading one is two boat lengths of the mark, then the outside yacht must give the inside one room to round the mark. The skipper of the inside yacht usually calls 'water please!' to make his claim.

The mark rounding rule does not apply at a starting mark, otherwise there would be nothing to prevent boats barging into the way of other competitors who are starting properly. It only applies at the windward mark when both boats are on the same tack, otherwise the basic port/starboard rule holds good. But at the leeward mark two boats may be on the same course but on different tacks. In this case the overlapping rule overrides the basic port/starboard rule.

Normally you are expected to steer your proper course, which is defined as the course you would sail in the absence of other boats to arrive at the finish as soon as possible. There is, however, one rule which excludes you from having to do this. This is called the luffing rule and it allows the skipper of a boat to defend his position by altering course away from the racing line to impede an overtaking yacht. He is even allowed to collide with it if his opponent refuses to give way. The reason for this rule is to cover what would otherwise be an unfair situation where the helmsman of a yacht to windward can easily overtake a yacht immediately to leeward by placing it in his wind shadow. If you wish to avoid being luffed pass well clear to windward, or go for the

leeward side. It is not recommended that a beginner should instigate luffs himself.

It is normal practice to trust each competitor to abide by the rules. If a collision occurs, or if a yacht with the right of way is impeded, then the offending yacht has to suffer a penalty. The standard penalty is being forced to retire, but, occasionally, the rules allow the offending helmsman to execute two 360 degree turns instead. Another alternative is for the offender to signal immediately his admission of error by flying flag I. The race committee will then apply a percentage penalty to drop the yacht down the finishing order.

If there is any doubt between the helmsmen as to who caused the infringement, they can both fly a protest flag and call a protest meeting. After the race each party states his case in front of a panel of experts, who will make a ruling.

**Diagram opposite: the essential rules of racing, where the orange boat has to give way.
Left: a fleet of racing dinghies on the course.**

Making a good start

Above: Flying Dutchmen dinghies starting from a championship line. It is important to find a clear wind. Already some boats are dropping behind.

To spread the fleet evenly along the starting line, a good committee tries to set it where there is no advantage in starting at one end or the other. In practice this is rarely achieved as the wind and current may alter at the last moment. The sharp helmsman watches both, and starts at the favoured end.

The first leg is normally a beat, so the favoured end of the line will be the one closest to the wind. To work this out, point the boat directly into the wind and sight the ends of the line so you can judge which is closer to the wind. *Diagram 1* shows a more accurate method which is to sail down the line with your sails trimmed perfectly. Then tack and sail back with exactly the same sail trim. If the sails flap, it indicates you are sailing towards the favoured end because you have to point higher into the wind to reach it.

Watch the water flowing round the marks and then weigh up the factors of tide and wind before choosing which end to start. Even if you

decide it is set fair, be prepared to revise your decision because the wind has a habit of changing at the last moment.

It is a good idea to practise part of the first beat, but never sail too far away from the line. Many beginners sail off for a quiet practice and then are not able to hear the starting signals let alone see them; or, they return too late, the wind drops and they miss the start.

You need to start your stop-watch at the warning gun and check it at the preparatory signal. You get a more accurate timing by watching for the gun smoke rather than waiting for the sound to reach you. If you are very sharp, you may be able to hear the race officer calling out the count-down to the gun.

Diagram 2 shows the method dinghy sailors use before a start, which is to lie stationary just behind the line. They know which is the most advantageous tack to start on, so they try to keep sufficient space below them. Just before the start they bear away into this space, haul in their sheets to pick up speed, and, with any luck, cross the line just as the gun goes. That bit of space is valuable and experts fight hard to keep their water clear.

Another technique is to come from behind the pack at high speed and hope to find a gap to blast through at the right moment. This is more likely to work if the line is less congested. It is the normal way to start in a larger boat which takes time to pick up speed.

In a cruiser fleet you will see the boats carefully timing their run in to the line. They will pick a point, such as a lobster pot buoy, or a transit on land, and time how long it takes to sail from there to the line. If the answer is say two minutes from the line, then they aim to turn and be at that spot heading for the line two minutes before (see *diagram 3*). This is not as easy as it sounds because the wind, and therefore your speed, is always changing. For example, the wind will almost certainly drop off just before the start due to the blanketing effect of all the other boats.

It pays to sail out to the course early, so that you have plenty of time to become adjusted to the conditions. If the first leg is to windward start on the starboard tack because you have the right of way. You should not be tentative and hold back. It is hard to recover from a bad start and you learn little sailing around in last place.

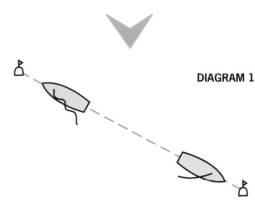

DIAGRAM 1

DIAGRAM 2

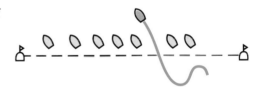

DIAGRAM 3

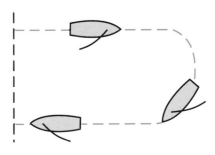

Right: 1, sailing down the line; 2, lying at the line; 3, timing a run to the line.

Racing to windward

DIAGRAM 1

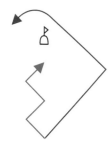

Above: one option is to steer to one side of the course, and then to tack for the mark. Another is to take short tacks up the middle.

After the start, concentrate on obtaining the maximum speed from your boat while steering as close to the wind as possible. This is difficult enough, but you must also be reviewing your race strategy. Before the race you will have decided which side of the course to sail. The wind may now have changed direction, and you may have been prevented from reaching the favoured side by other boats.

Choosing the most favourable side of the course
Sometimes it is obvious which side to take. For example, there may be more tidal flow on one side than the other. But remember that the tide changes. It could well flow with you on the first lap, yet be against you on the last.

An off-shore wind veers as it crosses the coast, an on-shore one backs. So it could pay to head towards the shore.

A sea-breeze usually swings round with the sun. When one is blowing it often pays to head off to the right hand side of the course to pick up the best advantage from this shift.

How to take advantage of wind shifts
There is often a rhythmic wind shift every few minutes, first one way and then the other. *Diagram 1* shows how the boat which tacks on these wind shifts can gain on one who does not. The rule is to tack when you are headed. You can use your compass to tell you if you have been taken off course and need to tack. If the wind shift is a lift, stay on the same tack, and make the best of it.

Often you will find that when it gusts, the wind changes direction. Do not tack, however, until you are sure the wind has headed you. A gust may sometimes shift the wind one way or another and then back again, so it pays not to be too hasty.

**Above: when crossing, remember port gives way to starboard.
Opposite top: try to keep your wind clear.
Diagram 2: the wind shadow extends for a considerable distance. Take action as shown to sail out of it.
Diagram 3: the wind from a leeward boat close in front can disturb the sails of the boat behind, which needs to tack to clear its wind.**

Do not be fooled by a lull in the wind. This brings the apparent wind forward, creating the illusion that the real wind has also altered. Maintain your course.

It is clear that the most scope for tacking on wind shifts occurs if you sail a middle course. If you tack up one side, there comes a time when you have no other option but to head for the buoy otherwise you will overstand it, i.e. sail past it.

Wind shadow

The sails of a boat to windward can blanket those of a leeward boat which is why the luffing rule is allowed. This wind shadow not only lowers the wind strength for the leeward boat, but the wind direction is altered enough for the leeward boat to be headed.

A wind shadow behind is triangular in shape and its length is at least three times the height of the boat's mast, probably more. And it extends in the direction of the apparent wind. So if a windward boat is within this distance from you, and you can see that its masthead wind indicator is pointing at you, then you are in its wind shadow. The closer you are the greater its effect.

It is not possible to overtake a boat while in its wind shadow. One alternative is to tack, but nearby boats sometimes prevent you doing this; in any case, the helmsman of the boat covering you can always tack too if he wants to keep you behind. Another option is to bear away from the wind and use your increased speed to break out of the other boat's wind shadow. The problem is that you lose ground to windward and you may decide that it is not worth it. In the end you have to weigh up all the factors, and, having taken action, hope you have made the right decision!

DIAGRAM 2

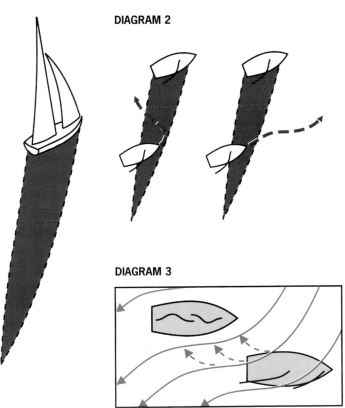

DIAGRAM 3

Rounding a mark

Rounding a mark is a test of your boat handling ability. You want to round smoothly, without losing speed. For example, at the leeward mark you should come in wide and aim to pass close to the buoy, so that you gain distance to windward (see *diagram 1*). A boat rounding untidily behind you will fall straight into your wind shadow. Keep the buoy in transit with its background, so you are aware of any tide that might sweep you onto it. Often there are other boats close to you when you round a mark, and this is when exciting situations develop.

At the windward mark, the port/starboard rules still apply when boats are on opposite tacks, and it is therefore safer to approach on the starboard tack (see *diagram 2*). The only trouble is that everyone else will be doing the same thing and as you come across the starboard lay line, you will have to find a gap to break through. If you tack in front of the others the chances are that you will be blanketed and will not make the mark.

At the leeward and reaching marks the special rule about rounding a mark always overrides the port/starboard rules (*diagram 3*). So it is to your advantage to be on the inside and establishing an overlap with the boat directly ahead of you. If you are successful in doing this at the point when he is at two lengths from the mark you should immediately make it quite clear to the outside boat that you wish to exercise your rights by calling 'water please'. If you are trying to establish an overlap at the leeward mark it pays to keep the spinnaker up as long as possible. Good crew work is critical here, because you certainly lose more than you have gained if you try to sail upwind with the spinnaker still raised!

There is no point in calling 'water' if there

Left: approaching the buoy at speed. Make sure you get your timing right. Below: rounding the leeward mark. Come in wide, exit close, and you'll finish on top!

is no room. Sometimes you see a solid mass of boats locked together at the mark with their skippers all calling for water. It is much more prudent to sail round the outside.

Before you round the mark you should have decided on your tactics for the next leg, so that you can position yourself immediately for a fast getaway. If it is a reaching leg, you may decide to head upwind of the fleet and then hoist the spinnaker and approach the mark on a broad reaching course. Or, alternatively, you may decide to head off to leeward of the other boats immediately which means your crew must be primed and have the spinnaker ready to hoist and, if possible, its pole in place.

DIAGRAM 1

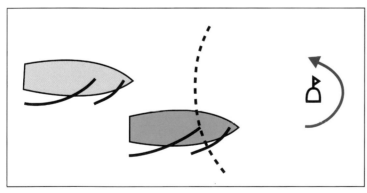

Above: if the inside boat has established its overlap in time it is entitled to call for 'water'.

DIAGRAM 3

Below: at the windward mark the normal port and starboard rules apply.

Above: chaotic situations arise if a large number of boats arrive at a buoy at the same time.

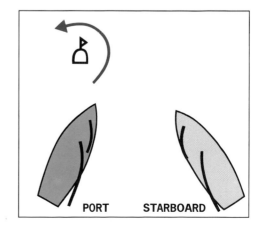

DIAGRAM 2

PORT   STARBOARD

Racing tactics

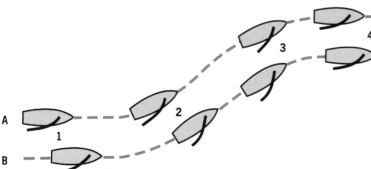

Diagram above:
1 The overtaking
boat (A) establishes
an overlap to
windward of B.
2 Boat B is now
entitled to alter
course and force A
to follow.

3 If the helmsman of
A draws level of the
mast of B he should
hail, 'Mast abeam'.
4 Boat B then has to
revert to its proper
course.

If you are sailing off the wind, you can place
your wind shadow over the boat ahead of you
which will enable you to catch him up. But if
you swing to leeward of him, or pass well to
windward, he will be unaffected. However, if
you pass close to windward, the skipper of the
other boat is entitled to defend his position. He
can luff into the wind as hard as he likes, and
you must keep clear. In fact, a well executed
luff can cause the overtaking boat to lose
considerable ground, although the luffing boat
will suffer to a certain extent, too. The luffing
boat can keep forcing you off course as long as
he remains ahead. His luffing rights cease when
the helmsman of your boat is level with his
mast. You can then hail 'mast abeam' and he
then has to revert to sailing a direct course to
the next mark.

Some points to remember

There are a number of principles about racing tactics that are too often forgotten in the heat of the moment:

1 It pays to be well prepared on-shore before you set off. You should have studied the weather forecast, the tide tables and read the race instructions.

2 You should get to the starting area in plenty of time, so that you can study how the wind is behaving. It is useful to practise a start, but remember to keep clear of any boats which may be starting ahead of you.

3 Be observant. You must always be aware of changing conditions. (Good crews constantly feed information to their skipper.) Watch the boats around you and compare your speeds. If they are gaining try to work out why.

4 Keep between the next mark and the boat astern. To windward, keep between him and the wind. Conversely, if you want to attack a boat in front, choose a different course.

5 The boat that wins is usually the one that makes the fewest mistakes. It often pays to sail steadily and not take risks.

6 Always try and keep your wind clear.

Above: coming up to the finishing line at the Royal Yacht Squadron in Cowes, these boats are keeping well in-shore to avoid the adverse tide.

Glossary

Aback Term used when a sail begins to fill with wind on the other side of it.

Abeam At right angles to the direction in which the boat is sailing.

Aft Toward the rear of the boat.

Airflow The pattern of the wind; its direction and strength as it flows around the sails. Also called windflow.

Amidships In the centre of the boat.

Apparent wind Combination of natural wind and wind created by the boat's forward motion.

Astern Behind the boat. An object, or the land, is said to be 'astern' of the boat. When boat's engine is in reverse and it is going backwards it said to be 'going astern'.

Backs When the wind shifts in an anti-clockwise direction.

Backstay Permanent wire that runs from the top of a boat's mast to the stern. See mast.

Bailer Container for bailing out water from a dinghy. A self-bailer does this automatically by sucking out water when a dinghy is under way.

Batten Strips of flexible plastic inserted in pockets at intervals up the leech of the mainsail

Beam The widest part of the boat. When particularly wide compared to length it is called 'beamy'.

Beam reach Point of sailing when the wind is abeam.

Bearing away When the helmsman turns his boat away from the direction of the wind.

Bias The direction of the weave of sail cloth which is diagonal to its weft and warp.

Block Pulleys used to obtain a better purchase on a rope.

Blue Peter Flag P in the International Code of Signals.

Boom Wooden or metal spar to which the foot of the mainsail is attached.

Bow The front end of the boat.

Broach or **broaching to** When a boat swings uncontrollably toward the wind when reaching or running.

Broad reach Point of sailing when the wind always blows between abeam and astern.

Buoyancy aid This supports the wearer in the water for a short time if a dinghy capsizes. Not designed to support anyone unconscious, and should not be confused with a lifejacket.

Camcleat a cleat with movable parts into which a rope is jammed to hold it.

Carve gybe Turn made at fast speeds by a windsurfer.

Centreboard Plate housed in centreboard case in the middle of the boat. It is hinged so that it can be raised and lowered by a rope. Its function is to prevent the boat being blown sideways when sailing close to the wind.

Centre of effort Theoretical central point in a sail, or a sail plan, through which the wind force can be said to act.

Centre of lateral resistance Theoretical point through which the sideways resistance of the centreboard, rudder, and hull can be said to act.

Chainplates Strong, metal fittings firmly secured to, and inside, a boat's hull. The shrouds, which help support the mast, are attached to them.

Class racing Where only boats within the same class compete.

Cleat A fitting around which a rope can be wound to secure it. To cleat is the action of securing a rope around or through a cleat.

Clew The corner of a sail closest to the stern of a boat.

Close hauled Point of sailing where the helmsman sails his boat as close to the wind as possible, usually about 45 degrees.

Close reach Point of sailing between a beam reach and close hauled.

Collision course When the compass bearing between two boats does not alter.

Compass bearing Lining up a compass with an object and taking the reading from the compass.

Cunningham Control which tensions the luff of the mainsail.

Daggerboard In dinghies, a type of centreboard which does not pivot and can only be adjusted vertically. Early sailboards were fitted with this type, and they had to be pulled out and carried when sailing off the wind. Modern sailboards have pivoting types, but the name daggerboard has stuck.

Dan buoy Tall pole, at least two metres long, with a flag on one end and a small buoy with a drogue on the other. Normally attached to lifebelts it is used to mark where the lifebelt is after it has been thrown into the water.

Downhaul On a boat it is a rope used to keep the spinnaker pole from rising too much.
On a sailboard it is the line which tensions the luff of the sail.

Downwind Sailing away from the wind.

Draft position The point of maximum depth in the curvature of a sail.

Fairlead An eye through which a rope

is threaded to guide it in a certain direction.

Fender Made of soft plastic and either round or sausage shaped, the fender is suspended against the boat's topsides to prevent damage when lying alongside.

Foot The bottom edge of a sail.

Foredeck Part of a boat's deck which is forward of the mast.

Forestay Wire which runs from a point on the mast called the hounds to the boat's bow. The jib is hoisted on it and it helps hold the mast in position.

Foreward Pronounced 'forrard' the front part of a boat.

Front The boundary line between warm and cold air in the atmosphere.

Genoa Large, lightweight foresail used in moderate weather.

Going about When, on a close hauled course, the helmsman turns into the wind so that the bow of his boat swings round until the sails fill on the other side.

Gooseneck Hinged pivot on the mast onto which the boom is fitted.

Goose-winging Putting the jib on the opposite side to the mainsail when the wind is directly behind the boat.

Gudgeons Metal eyes attached to a dinghy's transom and rudder. The pintles, or pins, on the transom and rudder fit into these which enable the rudder to swing freely.

Gunwhale Pronounced 'gunnel' – the edge of the hull or deck.

Guy Rope attached to spinnaker clew to which the end of the spinnaker pole is clipped.

Gybe When, with the wind behind, the boat is turned even further away from the wind resulting in the wind getting

behind the sails and the boom swinging across the boat. The opposite of going about.

'Gybe-oh' The command given by the helmsman to warn his crew that he is making a controlled gybe.

Halyard Used to hoist a sail, the top half is usually wire and bottom half rope.

Handicap racing Where different classes, and types, of boat compete under a handicap that depends on size, speed, and modernity.

Head The top corner of a sail.

Head to wind When a boat is pointing directly into the wind. Because the wind cannot fill the sails these will be flapping and the boat stationary or drifting backwards.

Heaving-to Manoeuvre where sails and rudder are adjusted so that the boat remains more or less stationary. Mostly used when the wind is too strong to continue sailing.

Heeling When a boat leans or tips because of the wind in its sails.

Helm The system by which a boat is steered. The crew member controlling it is called the helmsman.

Hounds Part near the top of the mast to which the shrouds and the forestay are fixed.

In stays When the boat does not have sufficient impetus to move through the eye of the wind when the helmsman tacks, and it remains head to wind.

Jib The foresail, or sail which is hoisted in front of the mainsail.

Kicking strap Also known as the vang, it is a rope attached to the boom and to the bottom of the mast. A system of blocks give it a powerful purchase

on the boom. It helps control the shape of the mainsail.

Land-breeze Off-shore wind which blows at night caused by the land cooling quicker than the sea.

Lateral resistance The water pressure on a lowered centreboard, also on the hull and rudder.

Leech Edge of sail closest to the back of a boat.

Lee helm When a boat's centre of effort and centre of lateral resistance are not balanced making it turn away from the wind.

'Lee-oh' Warning shouted by helmsman as he tacks.

Lee shore Term used when the wind is blowing onto a nearby coastline. Potentially dangerous in heavy weather or when an anchor drags.

Leeward The opposite side of a boat from which the wind is blowing. An object, or the land, can also be described as being to leeward

Leeway Sideways movement, or leeway, is most pronounced when sailing close hauled. Giving an object enough 'leeway' means you have compensated sufficiently to avoid it.

Luff The edge of the sail closest to a boat's bow.

Luffing up When the helmsman alters course towards the direction of the wind. Under certain circumstances, an allowable ploy when racing to prevent an opponent from overtaking.

Mainsail A boat's principal sail.

Main sheet The rope which, with blocks, controls the boom and therefore the mainsail.

Mast Wooden or metal spar on which the sails are hoisted. It is fixed firmly at its bottom end in a mast step and is held in position by shrouds and the forestay. Large boats also have a backstay. Dinghy masts are deliberately bent by various controls in order to alter the shape of the mainsail.

Match racing Where only two boats compete.

Neap tides Tides which have the least difference in height.

Off the wind When a boat is not sailing close hauled it is said to be sailing off the wind.

Off-shore Away from the land. A wind that blows from the land to the sea or description of yachts large enough to sail away from the coast.

One design racing Where yachts of the same class have to be identical when they compete.

On-shore On to the land. Description of a wind blowing from the sea to the land

On the wind When a boat is sailing close hauled it is sailing on the wind.

Outhaul Rope used to tension the foot of the mainsail.

Painter Rope used to secure a boat to an object. Attached permanently or temporarily to a boat's bow.

Pinching Sailing so close to the wind that the sails begin to lose their power.

Pintles Metal pins attached to a dinghy's transom and rudder.

Pitching Movement in a vertical plane.

Planing A manoeuvre by which a boat rises onto its own bow wave enabling it to exceed its theoretical maximum speed.

Pointing ability The ability of a boat to point closer to the wind.

Port Left side of the boat when looking towards the bow.

Port tack When a boat is sailing with the wind coming over its port side.

Pulpit Metal railings that surround a boat's bow above the deck. Lifelines run from it through stanchions on each side of the deck to the pushpit.

Pushpit Metal railings that surround a boat's stern above the deck. Lifelines run from it through stanchions on each side of the deck to the pulpit.

Reaching also **'on a reach'** Sailing when the wind is roughly abeam.

'Ready about' Command given by helmsman to warn crew he is about to tack.

Reefing Reducing the size of the mainsail.

Riding turn When a sheet is jammed on a winch.

Rig General name for a boat's mast(s) and sail(s). Hoisting a spinnaker, or altering the size of the foresail, does not alter a boat's rig.

Rigging General name for ropes, halyards, forestay and shrouds. The forestay and shrouds are known as standing rigging; the halyards, and the ropes which control the sails, as running rigging.

Roll tacking Advanced technique used to speed up a tack.

Rudder Detachable blade used with a tiller to steer a boat. A permanent fixture on larger boats.

Rules of the Road Legally defines which vessel has the right of way when sailing close to each other.

Running Point of sailing where the wind is blowing from behind a boat.

Sea-breezes On-shore wind caused by

the sun heating the land quicker than the sea.

Shackle U-shaped piece of metal through which a pin is screwed at its ends. Used to attach the halyards to the sails, etc. Also snap-shackles, or quick-release shackles; ropes with these attached can be quickly clipped and unclipped.

Sheet Ropes used to control sails. When you 'sheet in' you pull in on the ropes.

Shrouds Wires which support the mast. They run from the top of the mast, through spreaders, and down to either side of a boat's deck where they are secured to chainplates.

Skeg A small fixed fin at the stern. It helps keep a sailboard tracking in a straight line. On a large boat it sometimes supports the rudder.

Slot The gap between the windward side of the jib and leeward side of the mainsail, or the gap between the mainsail and the spinnaker.

Spars General term for mast(s) and boom(s).

Spinnaker Lightweight, triangular-shaped sail which is hoisted when a boat is running or, sometimes, when it is reaching.

Spinnaker sheet The rope attached to the spinnaker clew to which the end of the spinnaker pole is not clipped.

Spreaders These are attached either side of the mast to tension the shrouds.

Spring tides Tides which have the greatest difference in height.

Springs Ropes used to prevent a moored boat from moving forwards or backwards. One runs from the bow to a point on the shore close to the boat's stern and the other runs from its stern to a point on shore close to the bow.

Starboard The right side of the boat when looking towards bow.

Starboard tack When a boat is sailing with the wind coming over its starboard side and the boom is over the port side.

Stern The rear of the boat.

Streamers Strips of light sailcloth fitted to both sides of the mainsail at the leech to indicate airflow.

Tack The bottom corner of a sail closest to the front of the boat. Also, see tacking.

Tacking Same manoeuvre as going about. To reach a point in the same direction as the wind is blowing from, you take a series of tacks until you reach it.

Team racing When teams of three one design boats compete.

Telltales Strands of wool attached to either side of the jib at its luff used to check windflow.

Ties Strips of sailcloth used to tie lowered mainsail on to the boom.

Tiller Length of wood or metal which fits horizontally into the top of the rudder and used to control it. Dinghy tillers have tiller extensions to enable the helmsman to retain control when leaning out.

Topping lift Wire on larger boats which support the boom when the mainsail is not hoisted.

Topsides Surface of the hull above the water.

Transit When two posts or objects are in line vertically they are said to be in transit. Taking a transit is when two objects are lined up to ensure an anchor

is holding, or to maintain course.

Transom Flat area at the stern where rudder is attached.

Trapeze Harness and wire attached to mast used by crew to get his or her weight much further to windward than just leaning out.

Trim The balance of the boat fore and aft. Trimming the boat means ensuring that helmsman and crew are in the right position to maximise its speed. Trimming the sails means adjusting the sails until they are set correctly. A trimmer is one who trims the sheets.

Turbulence Occurs when the airflow around the sails is interrupted.

Twist A sail's shape which alters to correspond with the changing angle of the apparent wind.

Twisting off Happens when a gust hits the sail. The top twists away from the wind allowing the excess wind to escape.

Uphaul Line which supports and controls the spinnaker pole or, on a sailboard, rope used to pull the rig out of the water.

Upwind Towards the wind.

Vang See kicking strap.

Vector diagram Used to add up two quantities both in magnitude and direction.

Veers When the wind shifts in a clockwise direction.

Warp Rope used to secure a boat. Or the threads of sail cloth which are woven vertically.

'Water!' Shouted by helmsman when he is entitled to be given room to round a racing mark by the boat outside him.

Water start Method used by fallen windsurfers while still in the water to

bring the rig out of the water and start sailing.

Wearing round Manoeuvre which takes the boat from running on one tack to running on the other by bringing its bow through the eye of the wind instead of gybing. Only done when wind is too strong to make a controlled gybe.

Weather helm When a boat's centre of effort and centre of lateral resistance are not balanced, making it tend to turn into the wind unless a correction to the rudder is made.

Weft The threads of sail cloth which are woven horizontally.

Windflow See airflow.

Wind force The sum of all the pressures acting over a sail.

Wind shadow Caused when the sails of a boat to windward blanket those of a boat to leeward of it.

Windsurfer Someone who uses a sailboard. A sailboard can also be called a windsurfer.

Windward The side of the boat from which the wind is blowing. Also used as a direction so that an object, or the land, can be described as being to windward.

Wishbone boom This is divided into two and is shaped in a roughly parabolic curve. The sail is set between the two parts which meet at either end.

Index